THE BOOK OF ANCIENT BASTARDS

101 OF THE WORST
Miscreants and Misdeeds
FROM **ANCIENT SUMER** TO THE **ENLIGHTENMENT**

BRIAN THORNTON

Avon, Massachusetts

For Robyn

Published by
Adams Media, a division of F+W Media, Inc.
57 Littlefield Street, Avon, MA 02322. U.S.A.
www.adamsmedia.com

ISBN 10: 1-4405-2488-2
ISBN 13: 978-1-4405-2488-2
eISBN 10: 1-4405-2557-9
eISBN 13: 978-1-4405-2557-5

Printed in the United States of America.

10 9 8 7 6 5 4 3 2 1

Library of Congress Cataloging-in-Publication Data

Thornton, Brian
The book of ancient bastards / Brian Thornton.
p. cm.
Includes index.
ISBN-13: 978-1-4405-2488-2
ISBN-10: 1-4405-2488-2
ISBN-13: 978-1-4405-2557-5 (electronic)
ISBN-10: 1-4405-2557-9 (electronic)
1. History, Ancient—Miscellanea. 2. Biography—Miscellanea. 3. Good and evil—History—
Miscellanea. 4. Scandals—History—Miscellanea. I. Title.
D62.T47 2011
920.02—dc22
2011006235

This book is available at quantity discounts for bulk purchases.
For information, please call 1-800-289-0963.

ACKNOWLEDGMENTS

I've said before that the creation of a book is a collaborative effort. Such was definitely the case with *The Book of Ancient Bastards*. Paula Munier, Director of Innovation at Adams Media, believed in the project from the moment I brought it to her, and supported me every step of the way. My agent Gina Panettieri helped get me a deal and made it a better one. Development Editor Jennifer Lawler was a true professional and the embodiment of "grace under pressure." Thank you all.

And thanks to colleagues like author Jeri Westerson, who helped with the selection of bastards who occupy the medieval section of the book, and author/editor Heather B. Moore, for her help with the research on King Solomon. Your efforts helped make the book better, and for that, I am deeply grateful.

Lastly and most importantly, thanks to my family: my parents Hal and Berniece, and my brother Paul, for all of their support. And thanks most especially to my wife Robyn. Once again this book is dedicated to you.

CONTENTS

INTRODUCTION:.................................xiii

1. SARGON OF AKKAD:
Just Like Moses, Only Bloodier, and Not Egyptian (reigned 2334–2279 B.C.) 1

2. HAMMURABI THE LAW GIVER
Sometimes Your Really Don't Want to Lick the Spoon (reigned 1792–1750 B.C.)..4

3. AKHENATON:
Or How to Get Your Own People to Destroy Every Trace of You After You're Gone (reigned ca. 1351–1334 B.C.).......................6

4. RAMESSES II:
Or How to Make It Impossible for Your Own People to Forget You After You're Gone (reigned 1279–1213 B.C.)....................9

5. SENNACHERIB, KING OF ASSYRIA:
If You Can't Conquer Jerusalem, at Least Brag about All the Little Towns You Destroyed (reigned 705–681 B.C.)................. 12

6. KING SOLOMON:
All Those Women, All Those Gods, All That Trouble (ca. 1011–931 B.C.)... 14

7. NABONIDUS:
The Last King of Babylon and His Army of Gods (reigned 556–539 B.C.)... 16

8. DARIUS I, GREAT KING OF PERSIA:
Will the Real Usurper Please Stand Up? (ca. 550–486 B.C.) 18

9. POLYCRATES, TYRANT OF SAMOS:
Never Arm Your Enemies (reigned ca. 538–522 B.C.) 20

10. HIPPIAS, TYRANT OF ATHENS:
Just Because You're a Paranoid Tyrant Doesn't Mean Someone Isn't Out to Get You (reigned 527–510 B.C.) 22

11. ARISTAGORAS, TYRANT OF MILETUS:
Better a Live Rebel Than a Dead Royal Governor (?–497 B.C.).....24

12. ALCIBIADES OF ATHENS:
Opportunism, Anyone? (ca. 450–404 B.C.) 27

13. CRITIAS, LEADER OF THE THIRTY ATHENIAN TYRANTS:
Putting the Terror into Tyranny (460–403 B.C.) 29

14. DIONYSIUS I, TYRANT OF SYRACUSE:
When Philosophers and Tyrants Don't Mix (ca. 432–367 B.C.) 32

15. PHILIP II OF MACEDONIA:
Sometimes the Bastard Doesn't Fall Far from the Tree (382–336 B.C.)...35

16. ALEXANDER THE GREAT:
Bastard as Exemplar for an Age (356–323 B.C.) 37

17. OLYMPIAS, QUEEN OF MACEDONIA:
Sometimes the Bastard Doesn't Fall Far from the Tree, Redux (ca. 375–316 B.C.)..39

18. PTOLEMY I SOTER:
Sage Old Bastard Who Died in His Bed (ca. 367–ca. 283 B.C.) 42

19. PTOLEMY KERAUNOS:
The Guy Who Made Oedipus Look Like a Boy Scout (?–279 B.C.) ... 45

20. ANTIOCHUS IV EPIPHANES:
Why We "Draw the Line" (ca. 215–164 B.C.)...................48

21. PTOLEMY VIII EURGETES:
What Your Subjects Call You Behind Your Back Is a Lot More Important Than What They Call You to Your Face (ca. 182–116 B.C.) 51

22. CLEOPATRA THEA:
Poisonous Evil Queen or Just Misunderstood? (ca. 164–121 B.C.) ...53

23. MITHRIDATES VI OF PONTUS:
Gold-Plated Bastard (134–63 B.C.) 55

24. CLEOPATRA VII, QUEEN OF EGYPT:
Yes, That Cleopatra (69–30 B.C.) 58

25. LUCIUS TARQUINIUS SUPERBUS, KING OF ROME:
That's *Superbus*, Not *Superb* (reigned 535–509 B.C.) 61

26. HANNIBAL OF CARTHAGE:
Elephants and Siege Engines Just the Tip of the Iceberg
(248–182 B.C.) 64

27. GAIUS MARIUS:
The Man Who Killed the Roman Republic (157–86 B.C.) 66

28. LUCIUS CORNELIUS SULLA FELIX:
With Friends Like These . . . . (ca. 138–78 B.C.) 69

29. CATILINE AND HIS CONSPIRACY:
A Confederacy of Dunces? (108–62 B.C.) 71

30. LUCIUS CORNELIUS CINNA:
Lies and the Lying Liar Who Told Them (?–84 B.C.) 74

31. PUBLIUS CORNELIUS CETHEGUS:
When You Sleep with Someone, You're Sleeping with Everyone
They Slept with, Too (fl. first century B.C.) 76

32. PUBLIUS CLODIUS PULCHER:
With Friends Like These, Redux (93–53 B.C.) 79

33. MARCUS LICINIUS CRASSUS DIVES:
How Rich Is Rich Enough? (ca. 115–53 B.C.) 82

34. GNAEUS POMPEIUS MAGNUS:
If You're Going to be the "New Alexander," Better Prepare for a
Messy End (106–48 B.C.) 84

35. MARCUS TULLIUS CICERO:
No Fool Like an Old Fool (106–43 B.C.) 86

36. GAIUS (LICINIUS?) VERRES:
One Man's Thief Is Another Man's Art Connoisseur (ca. 114–43
B.C.) 88

37. GAIUS JULIUS CAESAR:
The Gold Standard of Bastardry (ca. 100–44 B.C.) 91

38. MARCUS PORCIUS CATO UTICENSIS:
The Bastard as Tiresome, Humorless Scold (95–46 B.C.) 93

39. MARCUS JUNIUS BRUTUS:
The Noblest Roman Tax Farmer of Them All (85–42 B.C.) 95

40. GAIUS CASSIUS LONGINUS:
"Lean and Hungry" Bastard (ca. 85–42 B.C.) 97

41. MARCUS ANTONIUS:
Dandy, Playboy, Ruthless Bastard (ca. 86–30 B.C.) 99

42. GAIUS JULIUS CAESAR OCTAVIANUS (AUGUSTUS):
Sage Old Bastard Who Died in Bed, Redux (63 B.C.– A.D. 14) . . . 101

43. LIVIA DRUSILLA:
Stage Mother for an Empire (58 B.C.– A.D. 29) 104

44. TIBERIUS CAESAR AUGUSTUS:
Bastard as the Grumpy Old Man Who Lives on Your Street
(42 B.C.– A.D. 37) 106

45. LUCIUS AELIUS SEJANUS:
Clearing the Way for a Monster (20 B.C.– A.D. 31) 108

46. CALIGULA:
You Call That Nag a Roman Consul? (A.D. 12–41) 110

47. CLAUDIUS:
When Is a Consul Like a Stone? (10 B.C.–A.D. 54) 112

48. NERO:
Actor, Singer, Poet, Athlete, Matricidal Mamma's Boy (A.D. 37–68) . .114

49. SERVIUS SULPICIUS GALBA:
How Being Too Cheap to Pay Off Your Promised Bribes Can Be
a Bad Idea (3 B.C.– A.D. 68) 117

50. MARCUS SALVIUS OTHO:
The Emperor as Scheming Pretty Boy (A.D. 32–69) 119

51. AULUS VITELLIUS:
The Fat Bastard Who Tried to Sell His Throne (A.D. 12–69) 121

52. DOMITIAN:
No Bald Jokes! (?–84 B.C.) 123

53. COMMODUS:
The Emperor as Hercules (A.D. 161–192) .125

54. DIDIUS JULIANUS:
The Man Who Bought the Roman Empire (A.D. 133–193) 127

55. SEPTIMIUS SEVERUS:
The Emperor Who Gave Us the Word "Severe" (A.D. 145–211) 129

56. CARACALLA:
Don't Drop Your Guard Along with Your Trousers (A.D. 188–217) 131

57. ELAGABALUS:
The Emperor and His Big Stone God (A.D. 203–222) 133

58. CARINUS:
How Screwing Your Employees' Wives Can Cost Ya! (ca. A.D. 250–285) 135

59. DIOCLETIAN:
The Best Place to Be Standing When Lightning Strikes Your Boss (A.D. 245–311) 137

60. CONSTANTINE THE GREAT:
The Next Best Thing to Being God (A.D. 272–337) 140

61. CONSTANTIUS II:
The Emperor as Paranoid Plodder (A.D. 317–361) 142

62. JUSTINIAN I:
When Nike Is More Than Just the Name of a Shoe (A.D. 483–565) 144

63. CHARLEMAGNE:
Literal Bastard, Figurative Bastard (A.D. 742–814) 146

64. EMPRESS IRENE OF BYZANTIUM:
Sometimes a Boy's Best Friend Is His Mother. This Isn't One of Those Times (ca. A.D. 752–803) 148

65. POPE STEPHEN VI:
Even Death Can't Stop Justice (A.D. ?–897) 150

66. BASIL I "THE MACEDONIAN" OF BYZANTIUM:
Why Trusting Your Life to an Assassin Probably Isn't a Good Idea (ca. A.D. 830–886) 152

67. BASIL II OF BYZANTIUM:
What It Takes to Earn the Title of "Bulgar Slayer" (A.D. 958–1025) 154

68. EADWIG OF ENGLAND:
Screwing His Kingdom Away (A.D. 941?–949) 156

69. POPE BENEDICT IX:
The Man Who Sold the Papacy (ca. A.D. 1012–ca. 1056) 158

70. WILLIAM I THE CONQUEROR:
Sounds Better Than "William the Bastard" (ca. A.D. 1028–1087)... 161

71. ODO OF BAYEUX:
When Your Vows Forbid You to Shed Blood, Use a Big, Heavy Club
Instead (ca. A.D. 1030–1097) 163

72. HENRY IV OF GERMANY:
How Much Penance Can One King Do? (A.D. 1050–1106) 165

73. WILLIAM II OF ENGLAND:
Red-Headed Bachelor Bastard (ca. A.D. 1056–1100) 167

74. ENRICO DANDOLO OF VENICE:
The Man Who Hijacked the Fourth Crusade (A.D. 1107?–1205):
....169

75. HENRY II OF ENGLAND:
Putting the "Devil" Into "Devil's Brood" (A.D. 1133–1189).......171

76. ELEANOR OF AQUITAINE:
Brood Mare to the Devil's Brood (A.D. 1122–1204)..............173

77. HENRY THE YOUNG KING OF ENGLAND:
Who Wants to Rule When There's Jousting to Be Done?
(A.D. 1155–1183)...175

78. RICHARD I THE LION-HEARTED:
A Talent for War (A.D. 1157–1199) 178

79. POPE INNOCENT III:
Don't Let the Name Fool Ya (ca. A.D. 1160–1216) 181

80. GEOFFREY II OF BRITTANY:
"That Son of Perdition" (A.D. 1158–1186) 183

81. JOHN I OF ENGLAND:
Short, Miserly, and Mean (A.D. 1167–1216) 185

82. PHILIP II AUGUSTUS OF FRANCE:
Cowardly, Duplicitous, and Effective (A.D. 1165–1223).........188

83. OTTO IV OF GERMANY:
Stupid Is as Stupid Does (A.D. 1165–1223)...................190

84. HENRY III OF ENGLAND:
A Saintly King with Locusts for Relatives (A.D. 1207–1272).....192

85. EDWARD I OF ENGLAND:
When the Only Tool You Have Is a Hammer, Use It on the Scots
(A.D. 1239–1307)...194

86. PHILIP IV THE FAIR OF FRANCE:
Don't Let the Name Fool Ya, Redux (A.D. 1268–1314)..........197

87. POPE CLEMENT V:
The Man Who Hijacked the Papacy (A.D. 1264–1314)...........199

88. KING EDWARD II OF ENGLAND:
Giving Away the Kingdom to His Boyfriends (A.D. 1284–1327) ... 201

89. ROGER MORTIMER, EARL OF MARCH:
Screwing the Queen Doesn't Make You King (A.D. 1287–1330) .. 203

90. PEDRO THE CRUEL OF CASTILE:
The Nickname Says It All (A.D. 1334–1369)................... 205

91. BERNABÒ VISCONTI, LORD OF MILAN:
Why Let Brotherhood Stand in the Way of Your Territorial Ambitions? (A.D. 1323–1385)................................... 207

92. CHARLES THE BAD, KING OF NAVARRE:
The Nickname Says It All, Redux (A.D. 1332–1387)........... 209

93. POPE URBAN VI:
Crazy Like a Pope (ca. A.D. 1318–1389)..................... 212

94. HENRY IV OF ENGLAND:
Why You Should Be Nice to Your Relatives (A.D. 1366–1413)..... 214

95. HENRY V OF ENGLAND:
Don't Let That Frat-Boy Act Fool Ya (A.D. 1387–1422)......... 216

96. TOMAS DE TORQUEMADA:
Grand Inquisitor, Closet Jew (A.D. 1420–1498)............... 219

97. LOUIS XI OF FRANCE:
The Spider King (A.D. 1423–1483)......................... 221

98. POPE ALEXANDER VI:
Chastity, Schmastity, I'm the Pope and My Son's Gonna Be a Cardinal (A.D. 1431–1503)................................... 223

99. RICHARD III OF ENGLAND:
Hunchback? No. Child-Killer? Probably (A.D. 1452–1485) 225

100. HENRY VII OF ENGLAND:
The Cheap Bastard's Guide to Solidifying Your Hold on Power (A.D. 1457–1509). 227

101. HENRY VIII OF ENGLAND:
Where to Begin? (A.D. 1491–1547). 230

Index 233

INTRODUCTION

When I wrote the original *Book of Bastards*, I pointed out the fact that no one is all good or all bad, that even Hitler loved kids and dogs, and that many truly "Great Men" of history had a touch of the bastard in them. As with American history (the subject area of the original book), so with the ancient world.

In fact, the ancient Greeks, who gave us such words as "history" and such notions as "democracy," also gave us the concept of the "hero." But where the modern interpretation of what makes a hero includes being on the good side of a given moral question, the original Greek concept of what makes a hero contains no such moral judgment.

For the Greeks, a willingness to risk and an impulse toward greatness was the major portion of what constituted a hero (that and of course the doing of great deeds, slaying of monsters, etc.). Such character traits can be found in spades among the ancient bastards in this book.

And while reptilian monsters such as Ptolemy VIII (a parricide who killed his own son, had him dismembered, and then shipped to his mother as a present) abound within these pages, there are, as was the case with the original *Book of Bastards*, plenty "Great Men" who showed plenty of innate bastardry in addition to (sometimes in support of) the great things they did in order to make names for themselves.

Perhaps that's part of the appeal. As I've written before, perhaps our own inner bastards respond to learning about the bastardry (usually on an epic scale) of those gone before. Because who doesn't love a good scoundrel and the scandals that attend them?

Either way, these are stories that we continue to tell hundreds, even thousands of years after those involved returned to the dust that spawned them. Say what you will about historical bastards—they've certainly got staying power!

★1★
SARGON OF AKKAD
Just Like Moses, Only Bloodier, and Not Egyptian
(REIGNED 2334–2279 B.C.)

> But because of the evil which [Sargon] had committed, the great lord Marduk [personal god of the city of Babylon] was angry, and he destroyed his people by famine. From the rising of the sun unto the setting of the sun they opposed him and gave him no rest.
> —The Chronicle of Early Kings

Imagine what it takes to forge a collection of petty, warring city-states into a unified, multiethnic empire. In a word: "bastardry"! Not necessarily out-and-out evil, but definitely bastardry.

Empire-builders down through the ages have been veritable poster children for the notion of "bastardry": Alexander, Caesar, Charlemagne, Napoleon, Hitler—the list is long. But who set the first example that so many conquerors have followed?

Ladies and gentlemen, meet Sargon of Akkad, the first bastard (but hardly the last) to build an empire through conquest.

Everything we know about Sargon screams "tough guy": his rise from humble origins to serve as cupbearer to the king of the city of Kish (a job not as effete as it might sound; it was an influential post in the ancient Near East); how that king grew to fear him and his popularity, so sent him to the court of a neighboring king in Uruk, asking that king to kill him, only to have Sargon overthrow the king of Uruk, turn around and go home to conquer Kish, and by extension, the rest of Sumer, Mesopotamia, and the Fertile Crescent all the way to the Mediterranean Sea. You don't get these sorts of things done without having a bit of the bastard in you.

---◟◞---

LEGENDARY BASTARD

Whether you're a devoted daily reader of the Bible or merely have seen the Cecil B. DeMille movie, you've likely heard this story: woman has baby, for debatable reasons woman decides to get rid of said baby, and rather than killing it outright, sets it adrift in a basket on a great river, hoping it will be found and taken in by some kindly soul. Moses, right? Well, yes, but the story of the foundling-who-goes-on-to-be-great is first told in the legendary birth story of Sargon of Akkad. In his case, he is the son not of an Israelite slave but of a temple priestess, and raised, not by the royal family of Egypt, but by a humble gardener. Still, the whole "baby in a basket in the river" thing is virtually the same (Sargon was adrift on the Euphrates, though, not on the Nile).

Willing to play politics, the man who became known as "Sargon" to us changed his birth name from whatever it was originally (we have no idea) to Sharru-kin (Akkadian for "rightful king"), a brilliant PR move, especially in light of the fact that Sargon was a usurper twice over (in other words, not the rightful king).

Once he'd built up his empire, the "rightful king" ordered the construction of a capital city from which to rule it: Agade. ("Akkad" was a geographic region in central Mesopotamia so-named for the people who invaded and settled there. "Agade" was the capital city that Sargon built.) So not just a conqueror, but also a builder. And more than that, a survivor. The king's own words show that he was most proud of that aspect of his personality. Sargon wrote in his autobiography: "In my old age of 55, all the lands revolted against me, and they besieged me in Agade 'but the old lion still had teeth and claws', I went forth to battle and defeated them: I knocked them over and destroyed their vast army. 'Now, any king who wants to call himself my equal, wherever I went, let him go'!"

Tough Old World bastard.

★2★
HAMMURABI
THE LAW GIVER
Sometimes You Really Don't
Want to Lick the Spoon
(REIGNED 1792–1750 B.C.)

If a man destroys the eye of another man, they shall destroy his eye.
—*Hammurabi's Code*

Hammurabi: a semimythical king of Babylon (a city-state in present-day Iraq) who handed down the first code of written laws more than 1,700 years before the birth of Christ. Hammurabi, the law-giver. Hammurabi, one tough bastard.

Let's face it, anyone who has ever been pulled over by a cop or spent a day in court (even if it's just traffic court) knows the open secret surrounding laws: those who make and enforce them are frequently bastards.

It's easy to forget that someone, somewhere, came up with the notion not just of justice but of punishment. And while Hammurabi certainly wasn't the first guy to mete out swift and terrible retribution for crimes real or imaginary, he was certainly the first one to make sure the rules of punishment got written down. In so doing, he intentionally codified quite a ledger of laws intended to protect both life and property. Unintentionally, he also preserved evidence of a fiendish imagination able to (with apologies to Shakespeare) "devise brave punishments" for the guilty.

The "eye-for-an-eye" punishment quoted above is a decidedly harsh penalty for an admittedly heinous crime, but "eye-for-an-eye" is a day at the beach compared to other rules laid down by Hammurabi in his code, including the notorious "trial by ordeal," wherein people suspected of a

4

crime underwent torture to assess their guilt or innocence. In one example, thieves were expected to lick a red-hot spoon, and then their tongues were checked to see whether they had blistered. If the blister burst when pressed by the judge with a finger, then they were found guilty; if it didn't, then innocent. Cold comfort when facing the possibility of having your taste buds singed off regardless of the verdict.

Hammurabi's Code is rife with examples of this form of "jurisprudence." For example, if a woman who sells wine in her establishment (and it clearly states that this applies solely to women) is charged with inflating the price of her drinks, "she shall be convicted and thrown into the water," meaning that the Euphrates River would be her final judge: if the woman floated, she was deemed innocent; if she sank, she was found guilty. Never mind whether or not the woman in question knew how to swim. Most people in the ancient Near East didn't! Another portion of the code that gave the Euphrates the final say stated that if a woman "leaves her husband, and ruins her house, neglecting her husband, this woman shall be cast into the water," and we all know how that turns out.

The code didn't require the Euphrates to mete out *all* ultimate penalties. Other methods were used as well: "if a 'sister of a god'[nun] opens a tavern, or enters a tavern to drink, then shall this woman be burned to death." What sort of bastard dreams up punishments such as these? Hammurabi of Babylon, that's who!

BASTARDS & SONS

Under Hammurabi's Code, fathers exercised enormous power within their immediate families. Fathers named their daughters' dowry price, and kept the money to use as they saw fit. Sons who struck their fathers for any reason had their hands cut off. Wives had some protection. If a husband tired of his wife, he could set her aside, as long as he gave her the price of the house he'd just turned her out of.

★3★
AKHENATON
Or How to Get Your Own People to Destroy Every Trace of You After You're Gone
(REIGNED CA. 1351–1334 B.C.)

> Akhenaton: the criminal of Amarna.
>
> —*Ancient Egyptian saying*

Akhenaton, the unexpected heir to the Egyptian throne, unsettled his people by glorifying one god instead of a pantheon. In return, they tried to pretend he never existed.

The "criminal of Amarna" didn't start out as a criminal, or even as a pharaoh. Likely suffering from Marfan syndrome, a disorder of the connective tissue (which would explain the elongated facial features and long, thin fingers on the statues of him that have come down to us extant), Akhenaton began life as a younger son of the great pharaoh Amenhotep III, whose rule lasted thirty-nine years, one of the most prosperous periods in Egyptian history.

Named Amenhotep after his father, the young boy was probably initially intended for the priesthood. But when his elder brother suddenly died, young Amenhotep became heir to the throne, and succeeded his father in 1351 B.C. as Amenhotep IV.

For five years his reign was fairly conventional. Then in 1346 B.C., everything changed.

Amenhotep IV changed his named to "Akhenaton" (which means "The servant of the Aton"), stating that there were no other gods, that the Aton (the Sun itself, as opposed to the sun-god Re) was the sole holy being, and that he himself, as pharaoh, was the Aton's voice on earth. Then he shut down the temples of the other gods, declared their priesthoods dissolved and illegal, and made it clear how things were going to be in his new order: He would worship and serve his god, the Aton, and the people of Egypt would in turn worship and serve him. Akhenaton even cleared out of the capital city of Memphis, taking his family and royal retinue with him, founding a new capital city in the desert, about 200 miles south of present-day Cairo. The ancient name of the city, Akhetaton, means "horizon of the Aton" or "horizon of the Sun." The city was later given the name "Amarna" by Bedouin tribes who settled nearby.

∽

ODDLY INSIGHTFUL BASTARD

Modern-day American presidents have made much of the fact that they live in a "bubble," insulated from contact with most of the people in their country, and talk about how they try to pierce that bubble, to be able to understand their people, in order to better serve as their leader. Not so Akhenaton. He embraced the "bubble," and if anything, made it harder to pierce. Not a very bright move for someone trying to make a sweeping fundamental change to a religious system that had flourished in the Nile Valley for millennia. In light of this, one of his homilies is oddly insightful, without demonstrating any actual insight on his part at all: "True wisdom is less presuming than folly. The wise man doubteth often, and changeth his mind; the fool is obstinate, and doubteth not; he knoweth all things but his own ignorance."

For the next decade, Akhenaton ignored his neighbors, didn't bother with diplomacy, and showed not the slightest interest in doing anything other than glorifying the Aton in his new capital out in the desert, out of touch with everything earthbound, a veritable hermit in the midst of his own people. In the end, it cost him his very identity as king of Egypt.

After he died, Akhenaton's subjects rebelled against his very memory, smashing his idols, abandoning both his cult and his new city, returning to

Memphis and to Thebes, and to the old gods and their temples. His very name was scratched out of every place in the country where it had been chiseled into stone, be it stele or monument.

Akhenaton himself faded from Egypt's memory for millennia. Quite a comeuppance for such a religious rebel bastard.

★4★
RAMESSES II
Or How to Make It Impossible for Your Own People to Forget You After You're Gone
(REIGNED 1279–1213 B.C.)

> His majesty slaughtered the armed forces of the Hittites in their
> entirety, their great rulers and all their brothers ... their infantry
> and chariot troops fell prostrate, one on top of the other. His maj-
> esty killed them ... and they lay stretched out in front of their
> horses. But his majesty was alone, nobody accompanied him...."
> —*Temple inscription, Luxor, Egypt*

The bit of boasting quoted above is nothing short of a public relations
move on the part of one of the most remarkable individuals to hold the
Egyptian throne, Ramesses II, who set out to do great things—and did.

Ruling nearly twice as long as any pharaoh before or after him, Ramesses II
began his reign in 1279 B.C. at the age of twenty-five. He ruled for over sixty-six
years, and died at ninety-one, either of an abscessed tooth (common in ancient
Egypt, where they had skilled physicians, but apparently not much in the way
of dental care) or cardiac arrest.

Incidentally, this is the first monarch in recorded history to get saddled
with the whole "the Great" nickname. Builder of cities and of monuments,
conqueror of foreign lands, Ramesses embraced being pharaoh with a gusto
seldom seen before or since.

At places such as Abu Simbel in Nubia (near the present-day border
between Egypt and Sudan), Ramesses erected colossal statues of himself for visitors from outside of Egypt's borders to see, admire, and most
importantly, be intimidated by. At home, he impressed his own subjects

in a similar manner with his massive temple complex at Karnak. He built a new capital city (named, of course, after himself) on the ruins of the former capital of the hated foreign invaders, the Hyksos, driven out of Egypt hundreds of years before his reign. The location was no coincidence: Ramesses was showing the world that Egypt was now invading the world, not the other way round.

∽

BASTARD (DOUBLE) DADDY

Ramesses had at least eight royal wives and any number of secondary wives, many of whom bore him children. Since Egyptian princesses were not allowed to marry anyone of lower social rank than they, it was common for them to marry brothers, cousins, even their fathers (in the Egyptian worldview, this form of incest merely doubled the "royalness" of any children born of two royal parents). Such was the case with Ramesses and the first of several daughters he married, Bintanath, who bore him at least one child. There were others! Cultural context aside, this little tidbit still makes you wanna say "Ewwww," doesn't it?

This is pretty funny in light of the fact that Ramesses's greatest military victory was actually his worst defeat. Early in his reign, he set out to reconquer foreign territories that had been lost to neighboring countries, such as Syria/Palestine to the north and Nubia to the south. It was in Syria, at a place called Kadesh, that Ramesses and his army, far from home, with their supply lines stretched thin, blundered into a trap set for them by their Hittite foes, an aggressive crowd who had extended their kingdom from Anatolia (present-day Turkey) into parts of Syria and Mesopotamia (present-day Iraq) and now threatened Egypt's frontier holdings in Palestine and Jordan.

What happened next—according to Ramesses—was a legendary victory. In reality, the Egyptian troops were routed. Ramesses signed a peace treaty, went home, and hyped the disaster as a great victory. In truth, he had lost thousands of troops in the slaughter at Kadesh, and this battle marked the end of his foreign military adventures.

Lying bastard!

★5★
SENNACHERIB, KING OF ASSYRIA

If You Can't Conquer Jerusalem, at Least Brag about All the Little Towns You Destroyed

(REIGNED 704–681 B.C.)

> Who was there among all the gods of those nations that my fathers utterly destroyed, that could deliver his people out of mine hand, that your God should be able to deliver you out of mine hand? Now therefore let not Hezekiah [King of Judah] deceive you, nor persuade you on this manner, neither yet believe him: for no god of any nation or kingdom was able to deliver his people out of mine hand, and out of the hand of my fathers: how much less shall your God deliver you out of mine hand?
>
> —*King Sennacherib of Assyria (attr.), 2 Chronicles, 32:13–15*

Sennacherib, the king of Assyria (in the northeastern part of present-day Iraq), rates a mention in the Bible for his siege of Jerusalem and other bastardry.

While the question of the sheer wickedness of the Assyrian people as a whole is open for debate, the bastardry of their kings is not. It is pretty much agreed that these guys were ruthless, fearsome, terrifying, and bloodthirsty.

Sennacherib was one of the worst. Not a conqueror himself, Sennacherib spent all of his time and energy consolidating the conquests of his father, Sargon II (reigned 722–705 B.C.). He consolidated vigorously and bloodily. When Hezekiah, the king of Judah (a kingdom in the southern portion of present-day Israel), refused to recognize Sennacherib's authority, Sennacherib conquered dozens of Hezekiah's cities and laid siege to Jerusalem.

The Bible states that Sennacherib only lifted his siege of Jerusalem after an angel of the Lord went out among the Assyrian army and killed 185,000 of them. According to Sennacherib, he only left because he had killed so many thousands of Israelites, carried off thousands of others into slavery, and stripped every city and town that fell before him. Oh, and then there was the massive indemnity that Hezekiah agreed to pay him: about 1,800 pounds of gold and nearly 5,000 pounds of silver, not to mention "diverse treasures."

Sennacherib didn't live long after receiving this massive bribe (he was murdered in 681 B.C. by his own sons). Nor, for that matter, did the Assyrian Empire. Assyria's neighbors, grown tired enough of the depredations of these fierce warriors, formed the first international war coalition in recorded history and wiped Assyria off the map in 612 B.C.

———————————— ✍ ————————————

BASTARD IN HIS OWN WORDS

After putting down rebellions against him in Babylonia and the western provinces (Phoenicia, Philistia, and Judah), Sennacherib did what most kings do after accomplishing a great feat: he bragged about it, carving boast after boast into a stone monument known today as the "Taylor Prism." It was the spin-doctoring of the day, and it reads in part: "Because Hezekiah, king of Judah, would not submit to my yoke, I came up against him, and by force of arms and by the might of my power I took 46 of his strong fenced cities; and of the smaller towns which were scattered about, I took and plundered a countless number . . . and Hezekiah himself I shut up in Jerusalem, his capital city, like a bird in a cage, building towers round the city to hem him in, and raising banks of earth against the gates, so as to prevent escape . . . ."

★6★
KING SOLOMON
All Those Women, All Those Gods, All That Trouble
(CA. 1011–931 B.C.)

> Wherefore the Lord said unto Solomon, Forasmuch as this is done of thee, and thou hast not kept my covenant and my statutes, which I have commanded thee, I will surely rend the kingdom from thee, and will give it to thy servant.
>
> —*1 Kings, 11:11*

Solomon, the famously wise king of Judah, proved less than wise in dealing with his own carnal appetites.

The favored son of the heroic King David, Solomon took the throne of Judah (a kingdom in the southern portion of present-day Israel) around 971 B.C. and ruled wisely and well for forty years. Stories abound of his sagacity in dealing out justice to his subjects, like the one about the two women who both claimed to be the mother of the same baby. Solomon ordered that the baby be cut in two, knowing that the real mother would beg him to give the child to the other woman rather than see the baby treated that way. He is also justly famous for ordering and overseeing the construction of the great temple that bore his name in Jerusalem.

Then, of course, there's the whole sex addiction thing.

See, Solomon liked women. (Whether or not they liked him back is not recorded.) During his forty years on the throne, Solomon collected a harem that would have been the envy of any Turkish sultan. According to the Bible, he had an even 1,000 women at his disposal: 700 wives and 300 concubines. And the wives weren't just any girls from off the street; they were princesses from neighboring countries married to Solomon by their fathers as part of any number of political alliances.

As if having that many women (plus the Queen of Sheba, whom he knocked up when she came to visit him) on the line didn't make him bastard enough, Solomon's harem proved to be a political headache. Not because there were 699 more wives and 300 more hookers in his household than might be socially acceptable, but because the wives, foreigners after all, had their own gods, and none of them was the god of the Israelites, who had so favored the fair-haired boy, Solomon.

Apparently it was only a matter of time before Solomon picked up many of these bad, idolatrous habits and displeased God. It was at that point that God told Solomon that he was going to break up his kingdom (in the quote at the opening of the chapter).

Some religious traditions hold that Solomon eventually saw the error of his ways, got rid of his idols (not sure about all those wives and concubines), and found redemption in the eyes of God. Muslims even hold that he never really fell away from his beliefs.

Pious bastard.

BORN-OF-SIN BASTARD

The son of David and Bathsheba, Solomon was the tangible result of David's great sin. When the king first met Bathsheba, she was already married to one of his most trusted soldiers, a man known in the Bible as Uriah the Hittite. Consumed with passion for her, David seduced her and got her pregnant, then arranged for Uriah's death in battle. Bathsheba lost her baby (according to the prophet Nathan, as punishment for the sin she and David had committed together), but she and David had a second son after they were married. That was Solomon.

NABONIDUS
The Last King of Babylon and His Army of Gods
(REIGNED 556–539 B.C.)

> The king is mad.
> —*The Nabonidus Cylinder*

So imagine you're the king of Babylon (a city-state in what is now Iraq), and three years into your reign, you decide to chuck it all and take off for a desert oasis where you join a cult devoted to worshipping the moon. Further imagine that you appoint your party-boy son prince-regent in your place. (After all, you're crazy, not stupid, you don't want to actually give up anything!)

Pretty wild story, right? Well, you know what they say: fact is stranger than fiction.

Ladies and gentlemen, meet the king in question: Nabonidus; the last king of Babylon, and his frat-boy son, Belshazzar.

Nabonidus's origins are shadowy; we know nothing about his father, but his mother was a priestess of the Babylonian moon god Sin (proper name, not to be confused with the English word for "religious transgression"). We do know that he came to the throne as a usurper, deposing and murdering the previous king, a child named Labashi-Marduk.

Presumably prompted by his mother's vocation, Nabonidus eventually went off to worship the moon, while his son stayed on to rule the kingdom. The Persians took the opportunity to make a run for the money and sent an army to Babylon. Nabonidus returned in time to see his son doing little to protect the city from the Persians. Nabonidus himself took command of the Babylonian army and went out to meet the Persians before they crossed his frontier.

He lost in battle, fled, and was later taken prisoner by the Persians. What happened next is uncertain. According to some sources, Nabonidus was burned alive by his Persian captors. Most sources agree that his life was spared and he was allowed to return to worshipping Sin.

And Belshazzar, the guy about whom the Bible itself remarks, "You have been judged and found wanting"? No one is really sure what happened to the guy after his dad surrendered.

Mysterious bastard!

―――――――――――――――   ♫   ―――――――――――――――

BASTARD POTTERY

When Nabonidus realized he had a full-scale military crisis on his hands, he left his oasis temple and returned to defend Babylon against the invading Persians. And he didn't go alone. He took an "army of gods" with him. In his mind, literally. To the Babylonians and many other peoples in the ancient Middle East (a notable exception being the Hebrews), gods were thought to inhabit the statues created in their honor. So when Nabonidus took every idol he could lay hands on with him to Babylon, he and all of his subjects believed that the gods were actually physically with him. It did him no good. The Persians kicked his ass, took the idols, and according to many sources put them back where they belonged. The Persian king, Cyrus the Great, boasted: "As for the gods of Sumer and Akkad which Nabonidus, to the wrath of the lord of the gods, brought to Babylon, at the command of Marduk, the great lord, I [Cyrus] caused them to dwell in peace in their sanctuaries, (in) pleasing dwellings. May all the gods I brought (back) to their sanctuaries plead daily before Bel and Nabu for the lengthening of my days, may they intercede favorably on my behalf."

★8★
DARIUS I, GREAT KING OF PERSIA
Will the Real Usurper Please Stand Up?
(CA. 550–486 B.C.)

> What is right I love, and what is not right I hate.
>
> —*Darius I*

The lines quoted above are part of a lengthy inscription carved into the side of a mountain in western Iran during the height of the Persian Empire. At first glance, they appear to be the words of a religious leader, or perhaps those of a noble and inspiring king.

They are neither.

These are the words of Darius I, Great King of Persia from 522 to 486 B.C., a usurper who likely had a hand in murdering his king and definitely had one in murdering that king's younger brother.

When the Persian king, Cambyses, set out on an expedition to conquer Egypt, Darius accompanied him, serving as a member of his personal guard. When Cambyses's younger brother rebelled back home, Cambyses left Egypt to return to Persia, dying under suspicious circumstances along the way. Darius was crowned king of Persia soon afterward, and led the dead Cambyses's army to Persia, where he dealt with Cambyses's rebellious brother by having him murdered.

Once he'd taken the throne, Darius proved initially unpopular. Several of his subject peoples rebelled. Babylon rose up twice. It took him years to consolidate his power.

Once he had done so, Darius found his western frontier attacked by the forces of Croesus, a wealthy king of Lydia (in what is now western Turkey).

But in this case wealth did not equal power, and Croesus lost in battle to the Persians, and Lydia became a Persian province.

Having conquered Lydia, Darius inherited not just Croesus's considerable wealth, he also inherited a conflict with the Greek cities of Ionia (a region in Asia Minor, now western Turkey). When the Persians conquered these Greeks, the Greeks bided their time for a bit, then eventually rose in revolt, killing their governor and driving the Persians out in 499 B.C.

Assisting these Greeks were their cousins across the Aegean Sea in the city-state of Athens. A furious King Darius ordered that one of his servants step up to remind him three times at every meal to "remember the Athenians." The king began plotting revenge on the impudent foreigners who had dared attempt to thwart his will.

Nursing his grudge for the several years it took to put down the Ionian Revolt, Darius massed the largest army the world had ever seen (the Greek historian Herodotus claimed that it numbered 250,000 men, but that's probably an exaggeration), loaded them onto boats captained and crewed by some of his Phoenician subjects, and set sail for Athens.

The famous result of all this grudge-holding came in 490 B.C. with the climactic battle of Marathon, where an army of Athenian heavy infantry, supported by soldiers from allied neighboring cities, smashed once and for all the myth of Persian military invincibility. And it was a fight almost completely of Darius the usurper's making.

BASTARD SPIN-DOCTOR

After Cambyses's death, Darius claimed that Cambyses had gone crazy in Egypt and died of natural causes on his way home to deal with his brother's rebellion. Darius then went on to claim that the man who rose in revolt against Cambyses was an imposter—not his younger brother at all. Some trick that, fooling his own mother and the wives in his harem!

★9★
POLYCRATES, TYRANT OF SAMOS
Never Arm Your Enemies
(REIGNED CA. 538–522 B.C.)

Without the knowledge of the Samians, Polycrates sent an envoy to Cambyses the son of Cyrus (who was gathering an army to attack Egypt) and asked him to send a messenger to him in Samos to ask for an armed force. When Cambyses heard this, he sent an envoy to the Samians and requested a naval force to join him in the war against Egypt. So Polycrates selected those of the citizens whom he most suspected of desiring to rise against him, and sent them away in 40 warships, charging Cambyses not to send them back.

—*Herodotus*, The Histories

In modern parlance, the word "tyrant" carries a negative connotation—it describes someone who rules in a cruel and arbitrary manner. But to the ancient Greeks who coined the word, it simply stood for someone who had seized power (usually by military force) and ruled alone, without necessarily being evil.

One of the ancient Greek tyrants who helped give the word its negative connotation was Polycrates, tyrant of the Greek island of Samos. While today he might be called an "enlightened despot" with a taste for literature, the arts, and great feats of engineering, Polycrates did terrible things to both his immediate family members and his subjects during his sixteen-year rule.

Seizing power along with his two brothers in 538 B.C., Polycrates initially split the island of Samos with the two of them. Within weeks, he had murdered one brother and exiled the other, taking total control for himself.

He enforced his rule with an army of Greek mercenaries. In order to pay this army, Polycrates levied a tax on any ship that passed within a few miles of Samos, which boasted a central location on the Aegean. Merchant ships either paid up to the captains of his fleet of triremes or had their cargoes seized.

Unlike many Greeks on the mainland, Polycrates maintained friendly relations with the Persian governors of the provinces that bordered his island. So when the Persian king Cambyses requested ships to support his invasion of Egypt, Polycrates sent him the ones mentioned in the quote that opens this chapter.

Once those sent by him to their certain deaths began to suspect they'd been betrayed, they turned around and tried to take Samos by force. When that didn't work, they set about preying on Samos's sea lanes as pirates.

As for Polycrates, his story doesn't end well. Believing that Polycrates had made a secret deal with the Egyptians, the Persian governor at Sardis had him seized and crucified.

Gruesome end for a gruesome bastard.

***

ENGINEERING BASTARD

Fascinated with how things worked, Polycrates harnessed the resources of his island home of Samos to produce the first trireme—a warship with three decks of oars, which allowed it to travel faster than standard biremes (which had only two rowing decks) and which made the ram it sported on its prow a whole lot more effective and devastating as a weapon. After the success of the first trireme, he had an entire fleet of them built. He also oversaw the construction of a great underground tunnel that acted as a pipeline, bringing a reliable supply of fresh water to the island from the mainland.

★10★
HIPPIAS, TYRANT OF ATHENS

Just Because You're a Paranoid Tyrant Doesn't Mean Someone Isn't Out to Get You

(REIGNED 527–510 B.C.)

> Hippias fled to Lemnos, where he died, the blood gushing from his eyes. Thus was his country, against which he led the Barbarians, avenged.
>
> —*Suidas, tenth-century Byzantine lexicographer and historian*

The last tyrant to rule ancient Athens, Hippias was a paranoid whose fear of plots on his life helped usher in the world's first democratic government (to replace his).

The son and successor of the most successful tyrant in the ancient world, Hippias became tyrant of Athens upon the death of his father Pisistratus in 527 B.C. Because he initially continued his father's policies (light taxes, no curbs on personal freedoms for the most part), the people were willing to let Hippias rule unopposed.

But Hippias had a brother: a patron of the arts and bon vivant named Hyparchus. And when Hyparchus got into a quarrel in 514 B.C. with a gay couple he was trying to break up (he had a crush on the younger and cuter of the two men), he wound up murdered.

At that point Hippias freaked out and began giving "tyranny" its more modern meaning. He arbitrarily killed those he suspected of plotting against him. He sentenced people to death for having the wrong friends. (And he seized their property for good measure.) The crackdown was swift and devastating.

In so doing, he played into the hands of the exiled Alcmeonid family.

These Athenians, run out of town by Hippias's father, promptly bribed the priestess oracle at Delphi to claim that the Spartans—backwards, superstitious, and with good reason the most-feared warriors in Greece—should invade Athens, take the city, and drive Hippias out in order to please the gods.

By 510 B.C. they had done it, trapping Hippias and his troops on the Acropolis, the city's fortified central hill. Settling in for a siege, Hippias at first seemed prepared to wait the invaders out. Then his family, including his children, fell into their hands (they had been trying to escape to Persia and were caught outside the city's gates). Hippias agreed to leave Athens and go into exile in exchange for the safety of his kids.

When he left Athens, Hippias, who had been a rare pro-Persian ruler in mainland Greece, hotfooted it to Persia and asked the Great King Darius I to intercede on his behalf. Darius allowed him to set up a government-in-exile in Persian-held western Anatolia (modern Turkey), but made him wait for a decade before sending emissaries to the Athenians demanding that they take back their tyrant and restore him as their ruler.

The Athenians laughed at him, then turned around and sent troops and ships to support the Ionian Revolt against Persia. See the entry on Darius I for the rest of the story.

∽

BASTARD'S END

Hippias served the Persians as an administrator and advisor for decades while awaiting the opportunity to be revenged on the city that had tossed him out on his ear. In 490 B.C., he felt he'd gotten it. By now close to eighty years of age, Hippias received permission to accompany Darius's invasion fleet to its appointment with destiny at the seaside plain of Marathon. Wounded in the ensuing battle, he died soon afterward, as noted in the quote from Suidas that opens this chapter.

★11★
ARISTAGORAS,
TYRANT OF MILETUS
Better a Live Rebel Than a Dead Royal Governor
(?–497 B.C.)

> While the cities were thus being taken, Aristagoras the Mile-
> sian, being, as he proved in this instance, not of very distin-
> guished courage, since after having disturbed Ionia and made
> preparation of great matters he counseled running away when
> he saw these things. . . .
>
> —*Herodotus,* The Histories

How's this for cynical: yesterday's tyrants becoming today's liberty-loving embracers of democracy? We've seen this during the modern era: Boris Yeltsin in Russia, for example, rejecting communism out of convenience rather than out of conviction, and being catapulted to power as a result.

But it's hardly a new story.

Take Aristagoras, the Persian-appointed tyrant of the semi-independent Greek city-state of Miletus (in the region of Ionia in Asia Minor, now Turkey), the guy whose push for homegrown democracy touched off the so-called "Ionian Revolt" in 499 B.C., a conflict that led to the loss of thousands of lives and served as the precipitating event in a wider conflict between the Greeks and the Persians over the two centuries that followed.

Hardly a born-and-bred defender of personal liberty, Aristagoras's opportunism was born of the most instinctive of human impulses: self-preservation. Here's how it happened.

Shortly after he became tyrant of Miletus, Aristagoras was tapped to help the empire pick up some new real estate in the form of Naxos, a strategically placed Greek island in the middle of the Aegean Sea. In exchange for helping with this, Aristagoras was to receive a large portion of the loot to be taken when the island fell.

In anticipation of said loot, Aristagoras took out a large cash loan from the local Persian satrap (governor). With this money, he hired mercenary soldiers and ships to help with the conquest.

The only problem was that Aristagoras got into a major personal feud with the Persian admiral set to lead the expedition. The feud got so ugly that the admiral secretly warned the Naxians of an invasion on the way. Not surprisingly, the whole venture failed.

BASTARD-IN-LAW

Aristagoras owed his position as tyrant to his father-in-law, Histiaeus. Histiaeus had been tyrant before him, and had done his job so well that the Persian king, Darius I, appointed him to his own governing council. When Histiaeus went east to the royal court at Persepolis, he recommended Aristagoras succeed him. Later, when Aristagoras was attempting to foment revolt among the Greek cities of Asia, Histiaeus secretly helped him, hoping that a rebellion led by his son-in-law would lead to his own being appointed to retake the city and re-establish himself as Miletus's tyrant.

But, in a setup that twentieth-century mafia bosses would admire, Aristagoras was still on the hook to the Persians for the money he'd borrowed. Desperate to save his own skin, Aristagoras set about quietly stirring a rebellion in Miletus and the neighboring cities, inviting such mainland Greek cities as Sparta and Athens to help their cousins across the Aegean Sea.

The Spartans, not surprisingly, refused (it was too far from home for these xenophobes). But the Persian king had just succeeded in really pissing off the Athenians by baldly interfering in their internal politics and insisting that they take back the tyrant (Hippias) to whom they had given the boot. So the Athenians agreed to send a fleet of ships to help.

And with that the Ionian Revolt was born. The result? Sardis, the westernmost provincial capital in the Persian Empire (and home base of the governor who had strong-armed Aristagoras in the first place) was sacked and burned by the Greek rebels. After a five-year-long campaign and the investment of much time, effort, blood, and money, the Persians put down the revolt.

And Aristagoras? Still fearing for his own skin, he relocated to Thrace (in the European part of Turkey), where he tried to establish a colony from which to continue the war against Persia. He was killed trying to strong-arm the locals (see how this sort of thing just keeps running downhill?).

★12★
ALCIBIADES OF ATHENS
Opportunism, Anyone?
(CA. 450–404 B.C.)

> Meanwhile I hope that none of you will think any the worse of
> me if after having hitherto passed as a lover of my country, I now
> actively join with its worst enemies in attacking it, or will sus-
> pect what I say as the fruit of an outlaw's enthusiasm.
> —*Alcibiades, quoted in* The Peloponnesian War, *by Thucydides*

A brilliant favorite student of the great philosopher Socrates and a gifted
politician and military leader, Alcibiades was also an opportunist of monstrous proportions, concerned more with his personal fortunes than with
the welfare of those he aspired to lead. This combination of ego and self-
ishness led him to betray his people to an extent that might have made a
Benedict Arnold blush.

By 410 B.C., Alcibiades had developed a reputation as a wild man who loved a
good party, in addition to his acknowledged talents as a speaker and political
leader. Elected to Athens's city government that year, Alcibiades gave a dazzling
speech in the Athenian assembly, laying out a bold plan for ending the ongoing
decades-long war with her longtime rival, the city-state of Sparta.

He succeeded in convincing the Athenians that the key to victory lay in
invading the island of Sicily and seizing the rich city of Syracuse. Swayed by
his compelling oratory, the Athenians voted in favor of his plan, and Alcibiades left Athens later that same year as commander of a massive Athenian
invasion fleet.

But enemies at home had him removed from his command and arrested
on trumped-up charges of desecrating several religious idols. In a snit, he
went over to the Spartans and told them in detail about his plan for attacking

Syracuse and suggested how they might thwart the Athenian battle plan and win the war. The quote above is from the speech he is supposed to have given exhorting the Spartans to accept his advice.

The intelligence Alcibiades provided the Spartans proved devastating to his country. In fairness, he probably didn't intend to completely cripple Athens, merely to bloody her nose enough that his political enemies would be swept from power and Alcibiades himself would be welcomed back into the city and into power at the head of the government.

He got it half right.

Alcibiades was welcomed back to Athens several times over the next five years, first after his enemies were pushed out (as he'd hoped) when the Sicilian Expedition failed. But it wasn't long before he was forced to flee the city. Once again he changed sides, this time going to the Persians, to whom he gave advice on how to keep the Greeks from uniting.

In the end, Alcibiades died while attempting to get Persian backing for a proposed attack on Sparta. Surprised in an isolated farmhouse in what is now Turkey, he rushed out into the night with just a dagger in his hand when his enemies set the place on fire and was killed by a hail of arrows.

Traitorous bastard.

BASTARD WITH A PEDIGREE

Alcibiades was a member of the famous Alcmeonid family, which included such distinguished citizens as Cleisthenes, who had helped rid Athens of the tyrant Hippias and founded its democratic government, and Pericles, who had run that same government wisely and well for the thirty or so years that comprise the city's golden age. After Alcibiades, no Alcmeonid ever held a position of leadership within the city again. That was no accident.

★13★
CRITIAS, LEADER OF THE THIRTY ATHENIAN TYRANTS
Putting the Terror into Tyranny
(460–403 B.C.)

> Let it not be in the power of Critias to strike off either me, or any one of you whom he will. But in my case, in what may be your case, if we are tried, let our trial be in accordance with the law they have made concerning those on the list .... [Y]ou must see that the name of every one of you is as easily erased as mine.
> —*Athenian politician Theramenes, quoted in Xenophon's* Hellenica

Playwright, poet, scholar, great-uncle of the famous Athenian philosopher Plato (and contemporary of Plato's even more famous teacher Socrates), Critias was renowned for much of his life as a writer whose work was in demand. He was even featured as the titular character in one of Plato's dialogues, *The Critias*.

Too bad he ended his life as a blood-soaked traitor to everything his city had once stood for, a classic example of conservative overreaction resulting in the loss of much life and property.

By 404 B.C., Athens had lost its decades-long war with Sparta. As a result of the humiliating peace treaty, the Athenian city walls were leveled, its navy dismantled, and a collection of thirty oligarchs who favored Sparta were placed in charge of the government. Critias, a follower of fellow Athenian bastard Alcibiades during the war, was named one of these oligarchs (known afterward as "The Thirty Tyrants").

Critias, a strong personality with lots of scores to settle and bitterness eating away at his very soul, soon embarked on a vendetta against anyone who had ever wronged him. What followed was a bloodbath, one of the first recorded political purges in history.

———————— ∽ ————————

BASTARD PLAYWRIGHT

"Religion was a deliberate imposture devised by some cunning man for political ends."

This quote is attributed to Critias and is cited over and over again as his position on the cynical use of religion by politicians for their own purposes. A popular author in his own time, he wrote on a wide variety of topics and in a broad range of stylistic formats: everything from tragic drama to history to political tracts to poetry to collections of popular sayings. Quite a well-rounded tyrant!

"Day after day," writes Xenophon, "the list of persons put to death for no just reason grew longer." For every person he denounced and had put to death, Critias received his confiscated property as a reward. When the Athenian statesman Theramenes protested that The Thirty ought to be careful about killing people so indiscriminately, noting that today's butcher is tomorrow's butchered, Critias famously responded with a statement that would be echoed for years afterward by politicians conducting similar purges: "If any member of this council, here seated, imagines that an undue amount of blood has been shed, let me remind him that with changes of constitution such things cannot be avoided." One of the first times a politician used some variation of the notion, "You can't make any omelet without breaking a few eggs!"

Critias went on to denounce his former friend Theramenes, calling him a traitor and enemy of both The Thirty and the Spartan troops who had placed them in power. After heated debate, Theramenes was dragged from the meeting and executed on the spot.

Emboldened by this silencing of their most vocal critic, The Thirty went on to denounce and execute thousands of Athenian citizens, seizing their property as they went. Within a year, the oligarchs had become such an object of fear and hatred that the people rose against them. Critias was killed in the fighting that followed, and his memory was justly damned in the minds of his countrymen for decades afterwards.

★14★
DIONYSIUS I, TYRANT OF SYRACUSE
When Philosophers and Tyrants Don't Mix
(CA. 432–367 B.C.)

> [Dionysius], taking offence at something [Plato] said to him ... ordered him to be brought into the common market-place, and there sold as a slave for five minas: but the philosophers (who consulted together on the matter) afterwards redeemed him, and sent him back to Greece, with this friendly advice.... That a philosopher should very rarely converse with tyrants.
> —*Diodorus Siculus, ancient Sicilian Greek geographer and historian*

If ever there was a piece of work to prove that one man holding all the levers of power is usually a lousy idea, it was Dionysius I, tyrant of the Greek city-state of Syracuse in Sicily. Originally a government clerk, Dionysius rose through the ranks to ultimate power based on his ability as a political, diplomatic, and military strategist. To balance this out, he was also arbitrary, capricious, cruel, and (perhaps worst of all) harbored literary pretensions.

Dionysius fancied himself both a poet and a philosopher, boasting "far more of his poems than of his successes in war," according to Diodorus. Poetry being a big deal in the ancient world, and Dionysius being the big man on campus in Syracuse, he surrounded himself with other literary and intellectual types, including Plato, who, as described in the quote opening this chapter, got sold as a slave in the public market for speaking his mind in the presence of the philosopher-tyrant.

In another example of why it's a bad idea for a creative type to be bluntly open and honest with a benefactor possessing no discernable sense of humor, Dionysius asked the poet Philoxenus what he thought of Dionysius's poetry. When Philoxenus answered candidly, Dionysius had him dragged off to work in the quarries.

Dionysius regretted the action once he'd sobered up, freed Philoxenus the next day, then invited him to dinner again. The wine flowed (again) and Dionysius asked (again) what Philoxenus thought of his poetry. In response, Philoxenus told Dionysius's servants to drag *him* off to the quarries. This time the tyrant laughed.

------------------------------ ⟋ ------------------------------

ONE-EYED BASTARD

Dionysius was particularly fearsome in battle. He'd lost an eye early in life, and as a result presented a ferocious image that struck terror in the hearts of his enemies. That terror was justified, as even in victory he could be a particularly ruthless bastard: In 386 B.C., Dionysius led his mercenary army in an attack on the Greek city of Rhegium (now Reggio, in southern Italy). After a protracted and bloody siege, the tyrant, who fancied himself a cultured and enlightened man, sold the entire population of the city into slavery.

From then on, and for the remainder of his time at Dionysius's court, Philoxenus promised that he would give truthful criticism of the tyrant's work while also never again offending him. He accomplished this by basically inventing the double entendre. Dionysius's poetry, according to Diodorus, was "wretched," and he had a taste for tragedy, so when Dionysius would declaim a poem with a sad subject, then ask Philoxenus what he thought about it, the poet would reply, "Pitiful!"

Dionysius is reputed to have either been murdered by his doctors to make way for his son to succeed him or to have died of alcohol poisoning from having drunk too much celebrating a win by some of his poetry at a festival in Greece.

And Philoxenus? He eventually left Syracuse and went on to write his most famous and successful poem, a comic piece called *Cyclops*, about the ridiculous passion of the mythical one-eyed monster for a beautiful goddess.

Most people assumed that he was making fun of his one-eyed former benefactor. If Dionysius wrote a poem about his feelings on the matter, it hasn't survived.

★15★
PHILIP II OF MACEDONIA
Sometimes the Bastard Doesn't Fall Far from the Tree
(382–336 B.C.)

O how small a portion of earth will hold us when we are dead,
who ambitiously seek after the whole world while we are living.
—*Philip II of Macedonia*

The hard-bitten, ambitious, and ruthless youngest son of an undistinguished royal house, Philip II of Macedonia was a usurper and military
genius who reorganized the army of his backward mountain kingdom and
in so doing changed the course of history. He also fathered and trained the
most successful conqueror the ancient world ever knew.

Born in 382 B.C., Philip had two older brothers and was deemed so expendable
that he was used as a hostage (a political practice during ancient times in which
two sides in any given conflict exchanged Very or Semi Important Persons after
the signing of a peace treaty, as guarantee of their future good behavior towards
each other). Thus, he spent years in the Greek city-state of Thebes while still a
boy, and carefully studied the organization of the Theban army.

After his return to Macedonia, a Greek-speaking kingdom situated in
the mountains and plains north of Greece itself, Philip soon found himself
regent for his nephew Amyntas IV, infant son of his older brother Perdiccas
II. In 359 B.C., Philip took the throne for himself, setting aside the young
king and declaring himself the rightful king. It was a naked exercise of power
and nothing else.

Moving quickly to modernize his army, Philip arranged to pay his soldiers, drilling them incessantly and converting what had previously been
feudal levies into the first truly professional nonmercenary fighting force

in the ancient world. For the next two decades, he campaigned every year, gradually expanding Macedonia's territory in all four directions, but especially to the south, toward mainland Greece.

In 349 B.C., Philip captured the city of Olynthus (in northwestern Greece), whose leaders had made the twin mistake of opposing him and housing two rival claimants to the Macedonian throne. In a preview of what his famous son would later do to those who defied him, Philip destroyed the city utterly and sold its surviving inhabitants into slavery.

By 338 B.C., Philip had conquered all of Greece and the rest of the Balkan peninsula besides. Then he got himself "elected" leader of the so-called "Hellenic League"(a loose collection of Greek city-states that banded together against the Persians). He announced his intention to invade the Persian Empire as revenge for the Persian burning of Athens 150 years previous.

But problems at home distracted him. He quarreled with his son and heir Alexander, who fled along with his mother, Philip's first wife, Olympias. Recently married to a much younger woman who quickly bore him another son, Philip disinherited Alexander, making his newborn son his heir. Philip was assassinated in 336 B.C. (allegedly with the complicity of both Alexander and his wild, scheming mother), leaving his infant son as "king" for all of about ten seconds before Alexander took the throne.

———————— ∽ ————————

ONE-EYED BASTARD, REDUX

Philip was famous for having lost an eye in battle. It supposedly happened while he was besieging the Greek city of Byzantium (modern-day Istanbul) in Thrace. It also supposedly occurred on the same day in 356 B.C. that his son and successor Alexander (later nicknamed "The Great") was born.

Alexander ordered all but those who had fled to the temples
to be put to death and the buildings to be set on fire. . . . 6,000
fighting-men were slaughtered within the city's fortifications.
It was a sad spectacle that the furious king then provided for
the victors: 2,000 Tyrians, who had survived the rage of the tiring Macedonians, now hung nailed to crosses all along the huge
expanse of the beach.

—*Quintus Curtius Rufus, Roman historian*

Held up throughout the ages as a shining example of both the great conqueror and the philosopher-king, Alexander III of Macedonia was considered by many to be the greatest monarch of the ancient world.

He was also a homicidal megalomaniac who developed a god complex
to go with a drinking problem, likely had a hand in killing his own father,
murdered one of his own generals in a drunken rage, conquered the Persian Empire, and unleashed the Macedonian war machine on an unpre-
pared world, resulting in the deaths of untold numbers of people.

Born to parents who could barely stand the sight of each other by the time he
came along, Alexander was in his teens and already trained as a cavalry officer
and a leader of men when his father, Macedonian king and bastard Philip
II, took a new, young wife, whom he immediately got pregnant. When the
girl delivered a boy whom Philip promptly designated his heir, Alexander and
his crazy snake-cult-priestess mother Olympias fled Macedonia for her native
country of Epirus (modern Albania), where they cooled their heels until Philip
was assassinated later that same year. Alexander and his mother probably had

a little something to do with that. Within weeks, Philip's new wife, her opportunistic nobleman father, and her infant son had all been quietly put to death. And then Alexander was on to Asia, leading an army that Philip had built, conquering territories left and right.

When he entered Egypt, the priests of Amun there hailed him as a god himself and the son of their god, a connection that played to both his vanity and his political need to lend legitimacy to his conquests (after all, who can argue with the reasons of a god-on-earth for anything he does?).

The further he got from Macedonia, the more binge drinking he and his senior officers did, and the worse Alexander's god complex became. One evening, he got into a drunken brawl with one of his generals, a veteran named Cleitus, who had saved Alexander's life in battle. In the heat of the moment, Alexander killed him on the spot.

Overcome with remorse once he sobered up, Alexander contemplated suicide but was talked out of it by his entourage, who convinced him that Cleitus was disloyal and since Alexander was a god, he was therefore infallible.

When he finally died of a combination of malaria and exhaustion at the age of thirty-three, Alexander left a changed world behind him. Whether or not it was for the better is up for debate.

TYRIAN BASTARD

Alexander and his army found the Phoenician port city of Tyre an island and left it a peninsula. Unwilling to bypass the city and allow its Persian-allied navy to harass his supply lines while he pushed into Mesopotamia and onward to Persia, Alexander had his engineers spend nearly a year building a causeway, then a road, in order to take the city. The Tyrians fought back ingeniously and heroically. Alexander responded with the actions quoted at the start of this chapter: thousands killed outright, over 13,000 taken as slaves—the mailed fist in the not-so-velvet glove of a conqueror.

★17★
OLYMPIAS, QUEEN OF MACEDONIA
Sometimes the Bastard Doesn't Fall Far from the Tree, Redux
(CA. 375–316 B.C.)

The night before the consummation of their marriage, Olympias dreamed that a thunderbolt fell upon her body, which kindled a great fire, whose divided flames dispersed themselves all about, and then were extinguished. And Philip, some time after he was married, dreamt that he sealed up his wife's body with a seal, whose impression, as be fancied, was the figure of a lion.
—*Plutarch, Greek historian*

Olympias was a princess of Epirus (modern Albania) whose father married her off young to Philip of Macedonia around the time Philip seized the throne. While it may not have been a love match, it was definitely a union between two extremely gifted, ambitious, and passionate people.

Doting on the son who ensured her power base at the Macedonian court (Alexander), Olympias grew cold toward her husband once it became clear that he had not the slightest interest in remaining faithful to her.

For her part, Olympias could be hard to take: tall, imposing, a force of nature with her temper and her strong will, she also made a point of creeping out the Macedonians with whom she came into contact, especially by playing up her status as a high priestess of an Epirot snake-worshipping cult. Soon she and Philip were barely speaking to each other, and Alexander, along with his younger sister Cleopatra (no, not that Cleopatra), was tugged back and forth between two very strong parental personalities.

Finally tiring of Olympias, Philip married a girl scarcely older than his own son, and soon got her pregnant with his child. When this new wife produced a baby boy, Olympias, Alexander, and many of their followers fled to her brother's kingdom of Epirus, lying low there for nearly a year before Philip was assassinated in 336 B.C. With so much to gain from her husband's death, and given her reputation for ruthlessness, it is beyond likely that Olympias had a hand in the plot that killed Philip.

<hr/>

WHAT'S IN A BASTARD'S NAME?

Originally named Myrtale, she took the regnal name of Olympias when her new husband's chariot won an event at that year's Olympic Games. Taking the name ensured that the honor of a Macedonian victory at the games would be celebrated for as long as people spoke her name.

<hr/>

The first thing Olympias did upon returning to the Macedonian capital of Pella was to have her rival and Philip's new son killed, along with the girl's father, a Macedonian nobleman who had set up the match hoping to inch closer to the throne and power himself. That wasn't the end. Anyone who posed a threat to her son's claim to the throne met with a quick and ruthless demise.

Within two years, the son on whom she so doted had gone to conquer Persia, never to return. Olympias was left at the Macedonian court, along with the general charged to run things in Alexander's absence, Antipater. The two quickly grew to hate each other.

Once Alexander was dead, Olympias strove mightily to get his wife, his mistress, and both of the sons they had borne him (Olympias's grandsons) safely home to Macedonia, where she could protect them and the dynasty. Olympias died for her cause, at one point invading Thrace (in the European part of Turkey) at the head of an army to try to free her captured grandchildren. When she lost in battle and fell into the hands of old Antipater's son, she got what she had doled out to so many others: execution. She was killed in 316 B.C., and with this formidable barbarian queen out of the way, Alexander's wife, mistress, and sons didn't stand a chance. They were each in their turn quietly murdered.

> [Ptolemy] built a temple in honour of Alexander, in greatness
> and stateliness of structure becoming the glory and majesty
> of that king; and in this repository he laid the body, and hon-
> oured the exequies [funeral ceremonies] of the dead with
> sacrifices and magnificent shows, agreeable to the dignity of a
> demigod. Upon which account [Ptolemy] was deservedly hon-
> oured, not only by men, but by the gods themselves.... And
> the gods themselves, for his virtue, and kind obliging temper
> towards all, rescued him out of all his hazards and difficulties,
> which seemed insuperable.
>
> —*Diodorus Siculus, Sicilian Greek geographer and historian*

The most successful of Alexander the Great's successor-generals, Ptolemy
I Soter ("Father") succeeded because he was shrewd, calculating, and able
to control the political narrative in an age when spin-doctoring was first
coming into its own. We're talking, of course, about the Hellenistic Age,
the period that began with the death of Alexander the Great in Babylon
(323 B.C.) and ended with the suicide of the last Hellenistic ruler, Cleopatra VII of Egypt, in 30 B.C.

During the three hundred years that make up the Hellenistic Age, a whole lot
of ambitious and unscrupulous people (all of them related by blood in one way
or another, frequently several times over) did a whole lot of awful things to each
other, and all in the name of furthering their own political aims.

The seemingly inevitable wars that followed Alexander's death are known
collectively as the Wars of the Diadochoi ("Successors"). In dizzying pro-

gression, this ruthless pack of scoundrels picked each other off, the survivors of each round of violence circling each other, looking for an advantage, making and breaking alliances as it suited them.

That's why the phrase "Hellenistic monarch" tends to be basically interchangeable with the word "bastard" for scholars who study the period.

⤳

BASTARD SON, BASTARD BROTHER?

Ptolemy is listed all over the historical narrative of the period as "Ptolemy, Son of Lagus." No further mention is made of Lagus anywhere except this brief mention as Ptolemy's father. His mother was a distant relative of the Macedonian royal house and the rumored one-time mistress of Philip, father of Alexander the Great. It is possible (perhaps even likely) that Ptolemy's actual father was Philip himself, making Ptolemy Alexander's bastard half-brother. This would help explain why a boy eleven years older than the young prince was listed as one of his childhood companions, and even went into exile with Alexander when the prince fled to Epirus shortly before the murder of his (their?) father.

When Ptolemy, childhood companion and advisor to the young Alexander, was offered a command as a royal governor in the aftermath of Alexander's death, he chose Egypt: rich, fertile, both a breadbasket and a gold mine, easily defended because the deserts that surround it made travel across them by large military forces nearly impossible. From there, he ventured out to steal Alexander's body from the caravan taking it home to Macedonia. This was a real political coup: control of Alexander's body, to which he publicly paid every possible honor, gave Ptolemy the opportunity to set himself up as Alexander's most legitimate successor. And this is what he did, for the most part settling back and allowing the successors to kill each other off for the next four decades.

Ptolemy's greatest accomplishment wasn't founding a dynasty that lasted for three centuries in Egypt, though. And it wasn't writing a history of his famous king, used by countless historians during the next millennium (thereby allowing Ptolemy to by and large set the narrative of not just Alexander's life story, but his own). His greatest accomplishment lay in doing what no other Diadochus managed to do: he died in bed, of old age. Truly a coup for a bastard in an age of bastardry!

★19★
PTOLEMY KERAUNOS
The Guy Who Made Oedipus Look Like a Boy Scout
(?–279 B.C.)

[T]hat violent, dangerous, and intensely ambitious man, Ptolemy Keraunos, the aptly named Thunderbolt.

—*Peter Green, historian and Classics professor*

In an age where the phrase "Hellenistic monarch" and "bastard" were interchangeable, one of the most notorious bastards on the scene was a prince who rebelled against his father, married his sister, murdered her children, and stole her kingdom. All this after stabbing a seventy-seven-year-old ally to death in a fit of rage.

Ladies and gentlemen, meet Ptolemy Keraunos ("Thunderbolt").

The Thunderbolt's father and namesake, Ptolemy I, has his own chapter in this book for a reason. But where the father was wily, the son was aggressive. Where the father plotted, the son acted.

In his eightieth year, with the question of succession pressing upon him, Ptolemy I gave up on his impulsive, hotheaded offspring. Instead, he chose a more sober half-brother (also confusingly bearing the name of Ptolemy) as his co-ruler and eventual successor.

Furious, Ptolemy Keraunos fled to Thrace (in the European part of Turkey) and the court of one of his father's rivals, Lysimachus. Ptolemy hoped to gain Lysimachus's backing in a war with his father. Lysimachus put him off with vague promises, but did allow the younger man to stay at his court (possibly so he could keep an eye on him).

However, intrigue boiled over, and eventually Ptolemy left Thrace (moving quickly) with his sister Lysandra. They went to Babylon (in modern-day

Iraq) to the court of Seleucus, by now the only other one of Alexander's generals still left standing. Seleucus assured the two that he would support their bid for Lysimachus's throne. (Lysimachus just happened to be an old rival of Seleucus's.)

Seleucus's forces triumphed in the resulting war. Ptolemy, who had fought on Seleucus's side, demanded Lysimachus's kingdom as Seleucus had agreed. And just as Lysimachus had, Seleucus put him off with vague promises.

Oops.

Enraged at having again been denied a throne he considered his by right, Ptolemy stabbed Seleucus to death, an act which earned him the nickname "Thunderbolt."

Ptolemy then slipped out of Seleucus's camp and went over to Lysimachus's defeated army. Upon hearing that Ptolemy had killed the hated Seleucus, the soldiers promptly declared him Lysimachus's successor and the new king of Macedonia. The only problem was that Lysicmachus's wife Arsinoe (who happened to be Ptolemy's half-sister) still held Cassandrea, the capital city of Macedonia. So Ptolemy struck a deal with her.

─────────────── ⌒ ───────────────

BASTARD MARRIAGES

Since the time of the pharaohs, dynastic marriage has been a political tool used by rulers to cement alliances and found dynasties. At no time was this practice more in fashion than during the Hellenistic period, when Alexander's generals married the much-younger daughters of their rivals, and married off their own children to yet others of their rivals' offspring. Such was the case at Lysimachus's court: the old man himself was married to one of Ptolemy Keraunos's sisters, a woman named Arsinoe, and another sister, Lysandra, was married to Lysimachus's son and heir from a previous marriage, Agathocles. This is almost as confusing as all those Ptolemys, isn't it?

Arsinoe agreed to marry Ptolemy, help strengthen his claim to the Macedonian throne, and share power as his queen. In return for this, Ptolemy agreed to adopt Arsinoe's eldest son (also named, not surprisingly, Ptolemy) as his heir.

You can guess what happened next.

While Ptolemy was off consolidating his new holdings in southern Greece, Arsinoe began plotting against him. She intended to place her eldest son (the one named Ptolemy) on the throne and rule in his name.

Once again furious (it seems to have been his natural state), Ptolemy killed Arsinoe's two younger sons. Arsinoe headed home for Egypt and the court of her full brother, Ptolemy-II-King-of-Egypt-not-to-be-confused-with-any-of-the-other-Ptolemys-listed-herein.

But Ptolemy Keraunos did not live to enjoy his throne for very long. In 280 B.C., a group of barbarian tribes began raiding Thrace. The Thunderbolt was captured and killed while fighting them the next year.

★20★
ANTIOCHUS IV
EPIPHANES
Why We "Draw the Line"
(CA. 215–164 B.C.)

After reading [the senate decree] through [Antiochus] said he would call his friends into council and consider what he ought to do. Popilius, stern and imperious as ever, drew a circle round the king with the stick he was carrying and said, 'Before you step out of that circle give me a reply to lay before the senate.' For a few moments he hesitated, astounded at such a peremptory order, and at last replied, 'I will do what the senate thinks right.' Not till then did Popilius extend his hand to the king as to a friend and ally.

—*Livy, Roman historian*

Gotta love this guy: a propagandist of the first order, his years in Rome had impressed him with the futility of fighting that resourceful people and of the importance of staying on their good side. A usurper (no surprise, considering how many Hellenistic monarchs were), he stole the throne from a nephew he later murdered after first marrying the boy's mother. Antiochus was remembered by the ancient Hebrews as the evil king whose coming was predicted by their prophet Daniel.

Antiochus was the son of Antiochus III, who ruled the Seleucid Empire (which included parts of present-day Syria, Turkey, Iraq, Iran, and Pakistan). Our Antiochus spent many years as a political hostage to the Roman Republic after a peace treaty between the two countries was established. After his father died, Antiochus's older brother, Seleucus IV, succeeded to the throne. Antiochus was

48

recalled from Rome, while Seleucus's older son was sent there as a more appropriate political hostage from the new king. When Seleucus was murdered, his older son was still in Rome. Antiochus took the opportunity to seize the throne, at first calling himself co-ruler. A few years later, he got around to murdering his nephew.

After consolidating his power base, Antiochus went to war with the much weaker neighboring kingdom of Egypt, all but conquering it before being confronted by the Roman ambassador, Popilius, who demanded that Antiochus withdraw from Egypt or face war with the Roman Republic. This is the source of the adage of "drawing a line in the sand" (as laid out in the quotation that opens this chapter). Antiochus did not step over the line, but retreated from Egypt.

WHAT'S IN A BASTARD'S NAME?

The third son of Antiochus III (the Great), Antiochus seized power after his brother Seleucus was murdered in 175 B.C. Looking to strengthen his claim to the throne, Antiochus married his brother's widowed queen, his own sister Laodice (the third of her own brothers she was forced to marry, and to whom she bore children!). He also hit on the idea of calling himself "Antiochus Epiphanes," which in Greek literally means, "Antiochus, the actual manifestation of God on Earth." Because he was a bit of a nut, many of his subjects took to calling him (behind his back) "Antiochus Epimanes," a play on his chosen nickname that means "Antiochus the Crazy."

By this time broke and really pissed off, Antiochus decided to loot the city of Jerusalem and its venerable temple on his way home to Syria. In his eyes, it was merely a way of catching the Hebrews up on their back taxes. The Hebrews didn't see it that way, and when rioting ensued, Antiochus made the serious mistake of trying to suppress the Jewish religion.

The reasonably foreseeable result was the famous Maccabean uprising. You may have heard of a traditional celebration called Hanukkah? Commemorates the rededication of the temple after Judah Maccabee kicked the Seleucid king's butt? This is that.

Later Seleucid kings agreed to allow the Hebrews their religious freedom and limited political autonomy. By that time, Antiochus had kicked off himself, dying suddenly while fighting rebels in Iran.

★21★
PTOLEMY VIII
EURGETES
What Your Subjects Call You Behind Your Back Is a Lot More Important Than What They Call You to Your Face
(CA. 182–116 B.C.)

> The Alexandrians owe me one thing; they have seen
> their king walk!
>
> —*Scipio Aemilianus, Roman politician and general*

That's right, another Ptolemy. But where the first of our Ptolemaic bastards was ruthless and shrewd, and the second was brave, intemperate, and violent, our third was a gluttonous monster who celebrated one of his marriages by having his new stepson assassinated in the middle of the wedding feast, and later murdered his own son by this same woman (his sister!) in a brutal and sadistic fashion.

A younger son of Ptolemy V, who didn't do the Ptolemaic dynasty any favors, this Ptolemy bounced around from Egypt to Cyprus to Cyrenaica (Libya) until his older brother (also a Ptolemy) died in 145 B.C. The dead Ptolemy's young son was crowned shortly after his father's death (taking the regnal name of Ptolemy VII) with his mother, Cleopatra II—no, not that Cleopatra—as co-ruler. In short order, our Ptolemy manipulated the common people into supporting him as king in place of his nephew, and managed to work out a compromise with his sister-also-his-brother's-widow wherein he married her and the three of them became co-rulers of Egypt.

Not only did Ptolemy then promptly have his nephew (and now stepson) killed at the aforementioned wedding feast, he seduced and married as his second wife the boy's sister, who also happened to be his own niece, and his wife's daughter (confused yet?), also named Cleopatra. (No, still not that Cleopatra.) This after knocking up the sister/wife/widow of his dead predecessor herself, siring a son named Ptolemy (again) Memphitis.

When the people of Alexandria eventually rebelled and sent Ptolemy VIII, the younger Cleopatra, and their children packing to Cyprus, Cleopatra II (the sister/widow/first wife) set up their son Ptolemy Memphitis as co-ruler and herself (once more) as regent. Within a year, our Ptolemy (Ptolemy VIII, if you're trying to keep track) had the boy, his own son, murdered. Pretty awful, right? Unspeakable?

No, that's what came next.

Once he'd had the child (no older than twelve) killed, Ptolemy VIII had him dismembered and (no lie) sent to his mother as a birthday present!

As if this wasn't enough, Ptolemy went on to retake his throne and share power with his first wife (yes, the sister/wife/widow whose sons he'd killed) until he died of natural causes after a long life in 116 B.C. Unspeakable bastard.

———————————— ∽ ————————————

WHAT'S IN A BASTARD'S NAME?

When he took the throne of Egypt in 145 B.C., our Ptolemy took the reign name "Eurgetes" (Greek for "Benefactor"). In truth he was anything but. Quickly tiring of his lying, his murderous rages, and his rampant gluttony, his subjects began to refer to him as "Physcon" ("Potbelly") because he was so fat. The quote that leads off this chapter references that physical characteristic as well as his laziness. Beholden to the Roman Republic for its support, Ptolemy VIII was forced to actually walk through the city of Alexandria (as opposed to being carted about in a litter) while playing tour guide to a visiting collection of Roman V.I.P.s, including Scipio Aemilianus, the author of the quote.

★22★
CLEOPATRA THEA
Poisonous Evil Queen or Just Misunderstood?
(CA. 164–121 B.C.)

As soon as Seleucus assumed the diadem after his brother's death his mother shot him dead with an arrow, either fearing lest he should avenge his father or moved by an insane hatred for everybody. After Seleucus, Grypus became king, and he compelled his mother to drink poison that she had mixed for himself. So justice overtook her at last.

—*Appian*, Syriaca

The evil queen meting out death and destruction to her own children before her own well-deserved death in the quotation excerpted above has a very famous name: Cleopatra. No, not that Cleopatra.

This Cleopatra was also born in Egypt, but about a century earlier than the more famous one. Her father, Ptolemy VI, used her as a pawn in his diplomatic chess match with his neighbors, the Seleucid dynasty in Syria. First, she was married off to a usurper (Alexander Balas), then taken back by her father and married to the heir to the Seleucid throne (Demetrius II). Then after this second husband became king and was captured by the Parthians, her father again intervened and married her to Demetrius's younger brother (Antiochus IX). When that brother was killed in battle, she was returned to Demetrius, recently escaped from ten years of Parthian captivity.

By these three men she had several children, including the next two heirs to the Seleucid throne (Seleucus V and Antiochus VIII Grypus). And this was finally her opportunity to stop being a pawn and start being a queen. It was through her children that Cleopatra Thea exercised power, first murdering her son Seleucus V shortly after he became king in 125 B.C., then ruling as regent for her other son Grypus while he was still a child.

By 121 B.C., Grypus had grown into his teens, and well aware of the fate of his older brother, he apparently knew better than to trust his own mother. So when Mama Cleo decided to try to slip him a poison mickey in a drink, he turned on her and had her drink it herself.

Done in by her own treachery, Cleopatra Thea died as she lived the majority of her life: at the hands of a close male relative.

WHAT'S IN A BASTARD'S NAME?

Cleopatra was a common name in ancient Macedonia; in fact, Alexander the Great had a sister by that name. And the Macedonian rulers of the Hellenistic state in Egypt glommed on to the name as a potential connection to anything related to Alexander. So just as there were countless Ptolemys coming out of Egypt, damn near every female born to the royal family there over the 300 years of Ptolemaic rule in Egypt was named, you guessed it: Cleopatra.

★23★
MITHRIDATES VI OF PONTUS
Gold-Plated Bastard
(134– 63 B.C.)

> [Mithridates VI] was ever eager for war, of exceptional bravery, always great in spirit and sometimes in achievement, in strategy a general, in bodily prowess a soldier, in hatred to the Romans a Hannibal.
>
> —*Velleius Paterculus*, Compendium of Roman History

Here's one for ya: a monarch in the vein of that fascinating bastard Alexander the Great. Equal parts paranoid and propagandist, a matricide who also killed his siblings, all while dosing himself with antidotes to build his immunity to poison, Mithridates VI, ruler of the Greek kingdom of Pontus (in what is now northern Turkey), was a thorn in the side of an expanding Roman military-industrial complex for decades until his death in 63 B.C.

King from the time he was thirteen, Mithridates did not actually rule until he turned twenty, whereupon he had his regent (aka "Mom") killed, along with his brother and sister for good measure. According to his carefully scripted life story, before this, he'd fled into the forest for fear for his own life (Mom apparently wanted him dead), where he lived for years, killing lions and strengthening himself to take his kingdom back.

This guy knew how to frame a narrative.

Mithridates's neighbors to the west consisted of a bunch of small post-Hellenistic Greek-speaking kingdoms, all of them dominated from afar by the Roman Republic. Beginning in 133 B.C. with the foundation of the

Roman province of Asia in central Turkey, the Romans had begun to gradually expand into the region, first ruling indirectly through existing monarchs, whom they would co-opt and then set up as puppets, and eventually integrating territory into their provincial system after they had their hooks dug deep into the local economy.

Rome had civilian contractors (the Halliburtons of their day) called *publicani* who did everything from road- and public-building construction to tax collection in these conquered and soon-to-be conquered territories. It was a system ripe for the corrupting, and in no time Roman governors were looking for excuses to annex more and more territory in the hopes of getting hefty windfalls from the publicani who would in turn get lucrative government contracts to strip the newly incorporated territory of its wealth and then build a lot of very expensive roads.

So when the inevitable happened and in 88 B.C. a Roman general named Manius Aquillius trumped up an excuse to pick a fight with the kingdom of Pontus, Mithridates correctly read simmering Greek resentment of these Roman leeches and set himself up as defender of Greek liberty. Aquillius had the triple misfortune of getting out-generaled and crushed in battle near the city of Protostachium, being caught and handed over to Mithridates, and of being the son of a former governor of Asia who had levied ruinous taxes (50 percent and higher) on inhabitants who turned out to have long memories.

GOLDEN-THROATED BASTARD

Never one to miss an opportunity, Mithridates had Aquillius dragged to Pergamum (a major city) on the back of a donkey, pelted with filth the entire way. Then, on stage in front of thousands in the city's gorgeous outdoor amphitheatre, he had him executed in a particularly grisly manner. The historian Appian tells us how: "Mithridates poured molten gold down his throat, thus rebuking the Romans for their bribe-taking."

In the decades that followed, the armies of the Roman Republic fought no less than three wars against Mithridates, eventually wearing him down and defeating his forces, then incorporating his kingdom into their foreign territories. On the run and trying to evade capture (and the subsequent march through Rome in chains as part of some general's triumph before being executed), Mithridates is reputed to have attempted suicide by taking poison. In a fitting irony, he proved immune to the effects of the drug and had to opt for running onto a sword held steady by one of his officers.

Gold-plated bastard.

★24★
CLEOPATRA VII, QUEEN OF EGYPT
Yes, That Cleopatra
(69–30 B.C.)

> I will not be triumphed over.
> —*Cleopatra VII of Egypt*

Cleopatra, the queen who made Rome tremble with equal parts fear, hatred, and awe. The last ruler of the last independent successor state of Alexander the Great's empire, she imposed her will not with military might or massed sea power (although she initially possessed plenty of the latter) but instead used her wits and outlasted or co-opted all of her political foes save one.

Although born in Egypt, Cleopatra was a Macedonian down to her toenails. And unlike so many other members of the Ptolemaic dynasty, she was smart, smart, smart. Succeeding her doting father at the age of eighteen in 51 B.C., she cut a remarkable figure. Fluent in nine languages (Latin, interestingly enough, not being one of them), she was the only Ptolemy ever to bother to learn Coptic, the language of ancient Egypt.

Rather than playing up her Greek bloodlines, Cleopatra emphasized her "Egyptian-ness," publicly and ostentatiously taking part in Egyptian religious rituals; dressing more like Nefertiti than like Athena, she styled herself the "New Isis," the living embodiment of the Egyptian mother goddess (something earlier attempted to lesser effect by that Seleucid bastard Antiochus IV). Her Egyptian subjects (if not always her Greek ones) literally worshipped her for it.

To Romans, she represented every ethnocentric prejudice they so despised about so-called "decadent Easterners." Married in succession to both of her younger brothers (likely never consummated, because propaganda aside, Cleopatra was, as far as we can tell, very choosy about whom she slept with), she waited to have a child with Julius Caesar, into whose bedroom she famously had herself smuggled by being rolled up in a carpet when he came to Egypt in 47 B.C.

Rarely apart after that for the remaining years of Caesar's life, the couple had a son (Caesarion), and both he and his mother returned to Rome with Caesar. Until the day of Caesar's death, Cleopatra lived with him in his villa in Rome, a symbol to his political opponents of Caesar's intent to be a king himself in his own right.

INBRED BASTARD

A direct descendant of Ptolemy I, Cleopatra VII was the product of centuries of inbreeding. The Ptolemaic dynasty had adopted the previous Egyptian royal policy of marrying royal children to each other (the idea being that royal children in Egypt possessed no other social equals on earth to whom they could be married, and if one royal parent made for a child blessed by the gods, then a child with two royal parents would be doubly blessed). Genetics being completely unknown at the time, the Ptolemys couldn't possibly know the likely outcome: a royal family who proved "selfish, greedy, murderous, weak, stupid, vicious, sensual, vengeful," in the words of one modern historian. In contrast, Cleopatra, the intelligent, shrewd exception who proved the rule, shone all the brighter. This fit in with her billing herself as "the New Isis."

Getting out of Rome one step ahead of a Roman mob after Caesar's assassination, Cleopatra settled in for a fight once back in Egypt. When summoned to a meeting with Rome's newest eastern warlord, Marcus Antonius, she made a grand entrance that entranced the loutish Antonius.

The two made common cause against Antonius's rival Octavian, and whether or not theirs was the passionate love match recorded by both history and Shakespeare, they had three children together. Also together they ruled the east for a decade, until finally forced into yet another civil war with Octavian, who defeated them at the battle of Actium in 31 B.C.

Within a year, the both of them had committed suicide; their children were either killed or adopted into the family of Octavian, and Egypt had become a Roman province.

Say this for Cleopatra, though: she didn't lack for either brains or courage, and she came within an ace of winning!

★25★
LUCIUS TARQUINIUS SUPERBUS, KING OF ROME
That's *Superbus*, Not *Superb*
(REIGNED 535–509 B.C.)

By this blood, most chaste until a prince wronged it, I swear, and I take you, gods, to witness, that I will pursue Lucius Tarquinius Superbus and his wicked wife and all his children, with sword, with fire, aye with whatsoever violence I may; and that I will suffer neither them nor any other to be king in Rome!

—*Lucius Junius Brutus (attributed by the Roman historian Livy)*

Tarquin the Proud ("Superbus" is Latin for "proud" or "haughty"), also known as Tarquin the Cruel, was the seventh and final king of Rome. Supposedly descended both from a noble Etruscan (modern-day Tuscany) and a Greek adventurer from Corinth, Tarquin was also, according to the Roman historian and propagandist Livy, a tyrant who ruled without either seeking or taking the advice of the Roman senate, a vicious, bloodthirsty conqueror who ordered up wholesale slaughter, and a murderer who conspired with his sister-in-law Tullia to kill his brother (her husband) and his own wife (her sister), then eventually the king (her father!)

Once Tarquin and Tullia had gotten rid of brother, sister, and father (namely anyone who could stand in their way of ruling Rome), they set about consolidating their power. The Etruscan kings who ruled before Tarquin are supposed to have been smart enough to listen to Rome's "advisory council" called the "senate," and thus have given at least the illusion that they gave a fig for what "the people" thought about how they were governed.

Not so Tarquin. He set himself up as an autocrat, ignoring the senate and ruling through military might alone. He was reputed to be a great conqueror, in addition to being a thief who stole both his wife and his throne through political murder.

When Tarquin's son Sextus raped a virtuous Roman matron named Lucretia, it was the beginning of the end. Lucretia denounced Sextus as a rapist in front of every male relative she had, then stabbed herself to death.

One of her relatives took up her dagger and vowed on the spot to raise a rebellion to drive the oppressive Tarquins out. The populace rose in response, and Tarquin and his family fled Rome, never to return. He died in exile a few years later, still fighting to retake the city he'd lost. Rome's leading citizens convinced the people to forego kings, and to found a republic instead.

And that relative of Lucretia's who vowed to finish what she'd started? Lucius Junius Brutus, one of the Roman Republic's founders and first consuls and the ancestor of fellow Roman bastard (and assassin of Julius Caesar) Marcus Junius Brutus.

Of course how much of this whole story is actually true is debatable. After all, Livy was as much a propagandist as he was an historian, and he's pretty much the only source we have for the period of Rome's founding.

Historical bastard.

——————————— ✆ ———————————

POPPY-SLAYING BASTARD

Livy tells the story of how Tarquin covertly conveyed his wishes to the son who had recently gained control of Gabii, a neighboring town, as to what Tarquin wanted him to do next in order to secure the hold of the Tarquin family on this new real estate:

"Tarquin, I suppose, was not sure of the messenger's good faith: in any case, he said not a word in reply to his question, but with a thoughtful air went out into the garden. The man followed him, and Tarquin, strolling up and down in silence, began knocking off poppy-heads with his stick. The messenger at last wearied of putting his question and waiting for the reply, so he returned to Gabii supposing his mission to have failed." On hearing of how Tarquin had responded by lopping off poppy heads with his stick, his son Sextus Tarquinius understood Tarquin's meaning all too well, and in response heads began to roll in Gabii. It was one of the first such bloodbaths in Roman history. There would be many to follow.

★26★
HANNIBAL OF CARTHAGE

Elephants and Siege Engines Just the Tip of the Iceberg

(248–182 B.C.)

I swear so soon as age will permit . . . I will use fire and steel to arrest the destiny of Rome.
—*Hannibal of Carthage*

Hannibal, the great nemesis of Rome, the Carthaginian general whose father forced him to swear the oath excerpted above, who went on to ravage Italy for twenty years, trying to take the city of Rome. Hannibal, whose name Roman matrons used as a proto-bogeyman to frighten their children into doing their chores and saying their prayers. Hannibal, who made good on his promise and fought Rome to a standstill for a generation.

Hannibal, the son of a great general, was raised to think strategically and to hate Rome reflexively. His home city of Carthage (originally a Phoenician colony) on the North African coast in what is now Tunisia had lost part of its far-flung trading empire to the Roman Republic during the First Punic War (264–241 B.C.), and Hannibal burned with a desire to make the Romans pay.

In 218 B.C., Hannibal took an army from Carthage's colonies in Spain through southern France and across the Alps, into Italy, where he intended to sack the city of Rome itself. The logistical problem for Hannibal was that most of the terrifying war elephants he'd brought with him from Africa died during the passage through the Alps, and he'd also been forced to leave most of his siege engines behind. Without them, he would never be able to successfully besiege Rome. And since the Romans controlled the seas, Hannibal could expect little in the way of supplies and reinforcements from Carthage, either.

So he lived off the land, looting and pillaging his way up and down Italy for years, then for decades, defeating the Romans in battle after battle, but unable to either draw them into a climactic battle in the open or breach Rome's thick city walls. And the more Hannibal raided their farms to supply his army, the less likely Rome's allied cities in Italy were to go over to Hannibal's side in this war. He literally could neither lose, nor win.

Hannibal was eventually drawn back to Carthage and the climactic battle he craved was his at Zama in 202 B.C.

He lost. In the resulting peace, Carthage, was stripped of all of her overseas territories and reduced to a barely independent shadow of her former self. Hannibal went on the run, hiring out as a mercenary general among the Greek kingdoms in the eastern Mediterranean, continuing to fight Rome. His efforts came to naught. With the Romans closing in on him, and determined not to be dragged back to Rome in chains, Hannibal committed suicide in 182 B.C.

SOMETIMES A BRIDGE IS MORE THAN THE SUM OF ITS PARTS

At one point in his back-and-forth struggle with Rome, Hannibal became so angry at what he considered Roman intransigence and duplicity that, according to the historian Appian, he "sold some of his prisoners, put others to death, and made a bridge of their bodies with which he passed over a stream. The senators and other distinguished prisoners in his hands he compelled to fight with each other, as a spectacle for the Africans, fathers against sons, and brothers against brothers. He omitted no act of disdainful cruelty."

★27★
GAIUS MARIUS
The Man Who Killed the Roman Republic
(157–86 B.C.)

The law speaks too softly to be heard amidst the din of arms.
—*Gaius Marius*

Gaius Marius was by any measure an incredibly successful fellow: transcending a humble birth in the Italian countryside to rise to the pinnacle of power in the Roman world, he was the only man to ever hold the consulship an unheard-of seven times. He was also a ruthless bastard who exploited his series of elected government positions to enrich himself and enacted laws that turned the Roman legions into a professional fighting force and made them completely dependent on the generals who commanded them. In Marius's army reforms lay the seeds of the Republic's inevitable destruction.

Incredibly ambitious, Marius wanted to establish himself as a permanent player in Roman power politics. In order to do that he needed three things: money, respectability, and influence. His career in public office combined with several successful military commands easily earned him the first two.

But wealth and respectability were of little consequence without influence. In 110 B.C., he got it the old-fashioned way: he bought it. He cut a deal with a proud-but-poor patrician family with impeccable blood lines, the Julii. Marius married one of their daughters and in return they got access to his considerable fortune.

Once he became consul, Marius prepared to put down the ongoing rebellion of a former Roman ally in North Africa named Jugurtha. In order to do this, he needed troops. The problem for the new consul was that the Republic's legions were all tied down fighting barbarians along the northern frontiers and Greeks in the east.

So Marius began to recruit from a new source: the poor.

Previously all Roman legionaries had been recruited from among land-owning peasants, people wealthy enough to provide their own armor and weapons. But these citizen soldiers were in short supply, so Marius made another deal. If the landless citizens who crowded into Rome's cities agreed to serve in the army, the Republic would not only feed, clothe, and pay them, it would also train them and supply their armor and weapons.

With this move, Marius created the famous "Marius's Mules": professional soldiers able to carry everything they needed on their backs wherever they went. It was a stroke of genius. Jugurtha's rebellion was crushed, and Marius's hold on power secured.

But this masterstroke had unintended consequences. Because their generals saw to their needs, even ensuring that they received a grant of public land for a farm of their own once they had served in the army for twenty years, Roman legionaries began giving their allegiance to their commanders first and to the Republic second.

——————————————— ∽ ———————————————

NEW BASTARD?

Marius was a novus homo (Latin for "new man"), someone born as a commoner who became a member of the nobility upon serving a term as consul (one of two chief executives of the Republic, who led the armies in battle and executed the laws made by the senate, in much the way a modern-day president does), which he did for the first time in 106 B.C.

Combined with the political ambitions of numerous wealthy aristocrats, all looking to make names for themselves and outdo each other, the Marian military reforms had the net effect of weakening the Republic's already shaky foundation. Marius himself spent the next twenty years in and out of power, intriguing along with the others until his sudden death at age seventy shortly after being elected to his seventh term as consul.

Ironically enough, it was the great man's own nephew who finished what he'd started with his military reforms. His brother-in-law Lucius's son grew up to finish dismantling the Republic, paving the way for the empire that followed. His name was Gaius Julius Caesar.

★28★
LUCIUS CORNELIUS SULLA FELIX
With Friends Like These . . . .
(CA. 138–78 B.C.)

No friend ever served me, and no enemy ever wronged me, whom
I have not repaid in full.
—*Epitaph of Lucius Cornelius Sulla Felix*

Born in 138 B.C. to a patrician family long on pedigree and short on money,
Lucius Cornelius Sulla grew up in a slum with the dregs of Rome for
neighbors. Over the course of his life, he would rise to the top of Rome's
political heap, eventually seizing absolute power as dictator, then pulling
the greatest escape of any despot in ancient history: dying of natural causes
in his own bed.

Sulla came of age in the Roman Subura, a notorious red-light district where his
neighbors numbered among them the usual collection of thieves, pimps, hookers, and murderers. While Sulla shared their daily existence, he was exceptional
in that he came from a prominent family. On top of that, he was smart enough
to get himself the hell out of the Subura as quickly as he could (an inheritance from a rich, older girlfriend didn't hurt). He held a number of public
offices that family connections helped him secure and demonstrated a talent
for administration and courage while leading troops.

By the time of the Jugurthine War (against a former Roman ally in North
Africa), Sulla had become the right-hand man of fellow upstart bastard Marius, making a name for himself in the bargain. In no time at all the two men
were rivals, with the older Marius ever more jealous of Sulla's successes.

The result? Civil war.

What Marius had started by making legionaries into professional soldiers loyal to the generals who paid them rather than to the empire, Sulla further advanced by using his army to besiege Rome, destroying the Roman Republic in everything but name, the culmination of which would be Sulla's appointment as dictator in 82 B.C.

Until that point, Sulla and Marius (and their supporters) jockeyed relentlessly for power, killing off each other's supporters (using a political tool called "proscriptions," in which people considered enemies of the state were singled out for execution), seizing their property, and redistributing it among their own followers. These newly enriched followers were so many dragon's teeth sown without much thought to the consequences of their coming to power: names like Cinna and Crassus, Pompey and Catiline would plague the Republic with their squabbling over who would succeed Sulla.

Before he retired, Sulla had the opportunity to have one of these young bucks put to death but was persuaded to spare the young man's life. In his memoirs, he later expressed regret for having spared the young man in question. "In this Caesar," he wrote, "there are many Mariuses."

It takes a bastard to know a bastard.

$\backsim$

BASTARD'S CIRCUS

During his entire life, Sulla never forgot where he came from. Even when he had reached the pinnacle of power as dictator representing the interests of the conservative *optimates* political party, Sulla liked to party, to drink, to carouse, and he didn't like to keep company with stuffy senators and their wives. Instead, he did his drinking with the lowlifes he'd met during his upbringing in the Subura. In fact, when Sulla retired to his country villa, he took his favorite "girlfriend" with him: a female impersonator named Metrobius!

Lucius Catiline ... had great mental and physical energy, but his abilities were perverted and destructive. From his boyhood he had reveled in civil war, murder, robbery, and public discord. ... His boundless ambition was constantly directed towards wildly fantastic and unattainable ends. After the dictatorship of Sulla he was possessed by a tremendous urge to seize control of the government and he did not in the least mind what methods he used, provided he obtained supreme power.

—*Sallust*, Catiline

Lucius Sergius Catiline was descended from one of Rome's most distinguished old families. Like his fellow bastard Julius Caesar, Catiline entered adulthood broke. And like many other young Roman aristocrats who refused to curtail their lifestyles to fit a budget during the first century B.C., Catiline soon found himself swimming in debt. Catiline threw his support behind fellow bastard Sulla, and as a result made a fortune dabbling in property sold at auction during that dictator's proscriptions. In one notorious case, Catiline killed his brother-in-law, hacked off his head, and carried it to the Forum, where he got Sulla to add the poor unfortunate's name to the proscription lists after the fact, then received the man's property in the bargain!

In the end, Catiline attempted a coup to topple the existing Roman state and install him as dictator.

Like such contemporaries as Cicero and Pompey, Catiline seems to have been impatient with the Roman system of advancement through long government service. Where the others cut a corner here and there (Cicero skimping on military service, Pompey on civil positions), Catiline seemed ready to toss the entire playbook.

He began conspiring to bypass the senate and seize power as his benefactor Sulla had done. In furtherance of this plan, he attracted to him (in the words of the historian Sallust), "Every gambler, libertine or glutton, who had frittered away his inheritance in play, debauchery or entertainment" to whom the notion of having his debts canceled seemed appealing. His co-conspirator Manlius began raising troops in the hinterlands, calling the poor, the debt-ridden, anyone interested in bettering their lot for a march on Rome like the one Sulla had staged twenty years before.

QUOTABLE BASTARD

When Catiline ran a fourth time for consul in 62 B.C., he did not simply attempt to win influence in the senate. Like Napoleon and Hitler after him, he took his case straight to the common people. He was quite open about this cynical attempt to use the common people to help him bypass the political process and catapult him to power: "I see two bodies in the state," he said in a speech shortly before the election of 63 B.C., "One thin and wasted but with a head. The other is headless but large and powerful. What is so dreadful about my becoming head of the body that needs one?"

It was the consul Cicero who finally called Catiline out, exposing him in the senate as the opportunistic rebel he had become. Apprised of Catiline's attempt at a coup (and intent to murder hundreds of people, including Cicero himself) by an anonymous letter, Cicero stood on the floor of the senate, pointed his finger straight at Catiline and asked, "How long, tell me, will you abuse our patience, O Catiline? How long still will that madness of yours mock us? To what evil end will your unrestrained audacity hurl itself?"

Catiline eventually cracked and fled the city, meeting up with Manlius and his ragtag army and "marching on Rome." They didn't get far. Catiline died courageously but futilely in battle against the legionaries that Cicero sent to bring him back to Rome in chains.

Opportunistic bastard.

★30★
LUCIUS CORNELIUS
CINNA
Lies and the Lying Liar Who Told Them
(? – 84 B.C.)

> Cinna went up to the Capitol with a stone in his hand and took
> the oaths, and then, after praying that if he did not maintain his
> goodwill towards Sulla, he might be cast out of the city, as the
> stone from his hand, he threw the stone upon the ground in the
> sight of many people. But as soon as [Cinna] had entered upon
> his office, he tried to subvert the existing order of things, and
> had an impeachment prepared against Sulla.
> —*Plutarch*, The Life of Sulla

The last days of the Roman Republic bred a crop of opportunists the likes
of which the world hadn't seen since the death of Alexander the Great and
wouldn't see again till the Bush administration. In any other era, a bastard
like Lucius Cornelius Cinna would have stood out from the crowd. In late
republican Rome, his stature was diminished in comparison to that of
truly nasty bastards like Marius and Sulla.

Cinna was that most mundane of bastards: a political opportunist with no hard
principles save the advancement of his own interests.

Building on the dissatisfaction of noncitizen Italian residents of the
Republic, Cinna managed to earn the support of Marius's powerful rival
Sulla as a compromise candidate for consul. But Cinna crawfished on the
deal, getting himself stripped of his consulship (the only time this ever happened during Rome's long history) and exiled, cast out of Rome like the
stone he'd thrown the day he took his oath in the Capitol.

Raising an army from among his noncitizen Italian supporters, Cinna invaded Rome, overthrew his fellow consul Octavius (a conservative who opposed him), then threw in openly with Marius. This allowed the old goat to return from exile and begin doling out political payback for grievances real and imaginary.

The result was one of the bloodiest chapters in Roman history, so bloody that Cinna finally decided to put a stop to it. He and his allies ambushed several of Marius's gangs of slave assassins, killing most of them and bringing Marius's purge to an abrupt halt. But the damage had been done. This reign of terror would not be the last endured by the city during the succeeding decades.

As for Cinna, you can hardly say that he profited by letting Marius loose on the Roman populace. He continued to intrigue, and for the next three years managed to set himself up as dictator in all but name, until he was murdered by his own supporters in 84 B.C.

――――――――――――― ᧕ ―――――――――――――

BASTARD-IN-LAW

Cinna's daughter Cornelia was married to one of ancient history's most famous bastards, a guy named Gaius Julius Caesar. Caesar was also the nephew of Cinna's political ally, the bloodthirsty Marius. These family connections put Caesar under a death sentence after Cinna was assassinated and Sulla (a political enemy of both men) became dictator a couple of years later. Sulla relented on the death sentence, provided that Caesar cast aside Cornelia and marry someone of the dictator's choosing. Divorce was common during this era, and it is a testament to Caesar's character that he refused the deal and went into hiding rather than give his wife up.

★31★
PUBLIUS CORNELIUS CETHEGUS
When You Sleep with Someone, You're Sleeping with Everyone They Slept with, Too
(FL. FIRST CENTURY B.C.)

Sulla was also joined by Cethegus, who had been one of his most bitter opponents, along with Cinna and Marius, and had been driven out of Rome by them.

—*Appian*, The Civil Wars

Not to be confused with a later Cornelius Cethegus (Gaius, likely a relative) who was the most dangerous of fellow Roman bastard Catiline's allies in the senate during his failed conspiracy, this Cethegus was arguably the most infamous (and successful) turncoat of the late republican period in Rome.

A member of the senate since at least 88 B.C., Cethegus had chosen the losing side in the civil war between Marius and his supporters on one side and Sulla and his faction on the other. After Marius lost that power struggle, his supporters rallied in the fortified city of Praeneste. In no time at all, Sulla's forces were besieging the city, and this was when Cethegus lost his nerve.

Sneaking out of the city and throwing himself on Sulla's mercies (a dicey proposition, as the future dictator was predictable only in his lack of predictability), Cethegus offered to change sides and serve in his army. Sulla, ever the cynic, demanded a higher price. In fear of torture and death (at best), Cethegus agreed to his devil's bargain.

Returning to Praeneste, Cethegus persuaded 5,000 Marian supporters that Sulla had promised them their lives if they left the relative safety of the city's walls. If they did so, Cethegus promised, on Sulla's behalf, their lives would be spared.

They weren't.

Sulla had all 5,000 butchered.

———————————— ∽ ————————————

A BASTARD AND HIS HOOKER

Cethegus parlayed his changing sides into several high-paying government jobs under a munificent Sulla during his dictatorship and after his boss's death. From there, Cethegus went on to decades of great success in the senate, where he became a power broker, reliably controlling the votes of a number of novus homo ("new man" = commoners) senators who looked to him for guidance. In fact, a decade after Sulla's death, with the Republic still at war with Mithridates, and the senate about to decide who would lead the latest expedition to the east in order to punish the recalcitrant king of Pontus, a follower of Sulla named Lucullus took an unusual step. He seduced Cethegus's mistress, a high-class prostitute named Praecia. She in turn used her considerable charms to manipulate Cethegus into supporting Lucullus for command of the army that was going eastward to fight Mithridates. Lucullus got the command, in large part thanks to Cethegus, went east, crushed Mithridates, conquering Armenia in the bargain, and making such a name for himself and reaping such riches that he was able to retire from public life on his return to Rome and live the life of a philosopher. Okay, a really rich philosopher. What Cethegus thought of this is not recorded.

═══

Given Sulla's reputation for brutality and the straightforward manner in which he went after his enemies, it is inconceivable that Cethegus had no idea what his new boss was up to when he agreed to talk several thousand of his erstwhile comrades-in-arms into walking to their own deaths. And he took the deal.

That alone makes him a bastard, by the standards of any day.

★32★
PUBLIUS CLODIUS PULCHER
With Friends Like These, Redux
(93–53 B.C.)

> Publius Clodius, out from his saffron dress, from his headdress, from his Cinderella slippers and his purple ribbons, from his breast band, from his dereliction, from his lust, is suddenly rendered a democrat.
> —*Marcus Tullius Cicero*

If ever there was a Roman politician who merited the description of gadfly, it was Publius Clodius Pulcher (whose cognomen "Pulcher" means "good-looking"—the cognomen, or third name, was a nickname Romans used to distinguish all those people with the same names from each other). The guy got his brother-in-law's own troops to mutiny against him, another brother-in-law's fleet handed over to the enemy, Julius Caesar divorced, Cicero banished, and himself ransomed from pirates for no price other than his (not-so-good) reputation.

A member of the patrician Claudius family, Publius Claudius Pulcher changed his name to the more plebeian-sounding Clodius to build his political reputation within the ranks of the *populares* political party, whose power base was with the common people. Unlike so many other populares politicians, Clodius actually led the common people in a work stoppage while campaigning against Mithridates VI (the ruler of the Greek kingdom of Pontus) under the command of his own brother-in-law, Lucius Licinius Lucullus.

Portraying himself as "the soldier's friend," Clodius negotiated terms with a seething Lucullus that ensured his soldiers would receive their due of land, booty, and plunder—and on a timetable, no less! Lucullus sent him back toward Rome just as quickly as he could.

———————————— ⟳ ————————————

NO-TALENT BASTARD PIRATE RANSOM

The early first century B.C. was something of a golden age for piracy in the eastern Mediterranean. Publius Clodius Pulcher, as had other young Roman nobles before him, fell into the hands of pirates intent on ransoming him. Sending a message to the king of Cyprus (Rome's closest ally) requesting he ransom him, Clodius expected the standard fee of twenty talents (a little over 1,400 pounds) of gold to be sent for him, since he was a member of one of Rome's richest families. Much to Clodius's embarrassment, the king of Cyprus only sent two talents (a little over 140 pounds) of gold in response. It struck his pirate captors as so funny that this arrogant young Roman could not command so much as his own weight in gold that they set him free without taking anything. Tongues wagged around Rome for years afterward that the only price Clodius paid to be free of captivity was his anal virginity. Several years later, Clodius succeeded in getting the Cypriot king who had so undervalued him deposed and Cyprus converted into a outright Roman possession.

On the way home, Clodius also got himself appointed commander of another brother-in-law's fleet of Roman ships, which he promptly lost in battle, getting taken prisoner by the aforementioned pirates in the process.

Back in Rome, Clodius quickly acquired a reputation as a rake, bedding several married women in succession, including the wife of the still-absent Lucullus!

A longtime foe of the politician Cicero, Clodius succeeded in getting the great orator exiled (and his expensive hilltop mansion demolished) after Cicero had him put on trial for alleged incest with his own sister. Clodius's friend and benefactor, the wealthy Marcus Crassus, got Pulcher off by bribing the jury.

Often a precipitator of street gang violence, Pulcher fell victim to it himself at the hands of the slaves of a rival named Milo in 53 B.C., who stabbed him to death in the street. The result: all hell broke loose. Clodius's supporters took his body straight into the heart of the Senate House, that symbol of conservative *optimates* patrician power, built a funeral pyre for him within it, and burned the Senate House down in the process. You can't help but think how much that showboater Clodius would have appreciated such a spectacle!

★33★
MARCUS LICINIUS CRASSUS DIVES
How Rich Is Rich Enough?
(CA. 115–53 B.C.)

> O vile, worthless man!
>
> —*Marcus Tullius Cicero*

The irony of the phrase quoted above is that the words were written about the wealthiest man in Rome. Marcus Licinius Crassus Dives ("Dives" being a Latin nickname meaning "rich") was born to money, lost it in the proscriptions that marked the first phase of Rome's civil wars, and made it all back and more by taking cynical advantage of those same proscriptions to dispossess other wealthy unfortunates.

Crassus's father and brother were killed in a purge, and the family's considerable property was forfeited to the state, which promptly auctioned it off. It was a lesson the young Crassus never forgot. Coming of age as a supporter of the ruthless, ultimately successful dictator Sulla, Crassus was able to profit from exploiting the system that had dispossessed him when his own family's enemies had held the levers of power. He quickly amassed a considerable fortune, but that was only a start.

Crassus rapidly branched out into real estate and slave trading, two booming businesses during the late republican era. He was soon the wealthiest man in Rome and, by extension, the entire Mediterranean world.

But wealth was not an end in itself to a Roman like Crassus. Rather, it was a means to an end: power. It was Crassus who eventually put down Spartacus's slave revolt, hoping for a triumph in the Forum. It was Crassus who bribed Roman judges and juries in order to ensure his supporters escaped punishment for their crimes, and Crassus who got a piece of damned near every bit of trading action that took place in republican Rome. It was Crassus who bankrolled a young, ambitious, and flat-broke politician named Julius Caesar in order to bind the younger man to him. It was Crassus who served as the banker in the first triumvirate with Caesar and Pompey.

And it was Crassus who jockeyed for position with the other triumvirs, bargaining with them to be selected to lead a Roman army east to fight the Persians on Rome's frontier, hoping, even in his early sixties, to win military glory and with it more permanent political power. In 54 B.C., he got his wish. Too bad his army was crushed at a place called Carrhae.

― ∾ ―

HISTORY REPEATS ITSELF

When Crassus got himself captured at Carrhae, the Persians, cognizant of how their neighbor Mithridates VI had executed a corrupt Roman governor a few decades earlier, copied his methods. Mindful of the wealth of the man they had captured, they dispatched "Crassus the Rich" by, fittingly, pouring molten gold down his throat.

★34★
GNAEUS POMPEIUS MAGNUS
If You're Going to be the "New Alexander," Better Prepare for a Messy End
(106–48 B.C.)

> [Pompey] does not know how to win a war.
> —*Gaius Julius Caesar, after the battle of Dhyrrachium*

Gnaeus Pompeius Magnus (known in English as "Pompey the Great") dreamed of aping and even exceeding the deeds of celebrated Macedonian bastard Alexander the Great on the battlefield. Unfortunately, he was, in the words of one contemporary, "the vilest man alive." The kid first made his mark at the tender age of twenty-three in 83 B.C., raising private legions of soldiers, paying them out of his own pocket, and supporting Sulla in his attempts to wipe out the last of his opponents, the supporters of Gaius Marius.

Bypassing the traditional Roman steps to public greatness (holding offices such as aedile, questor, and consul) and still employing his own private army, Pompey went on to quickly win a string of bloody victories against Marian adherents from Sicily to North Africa, all before he turned twenty-six. So ruthless was the young man that his opponents gave him the nickname "adulescens carnifex": "teenaged butcher."

Next came a ten-year war to suppress a rebellion in Spain; after that, he swept the Mediterranean clean of the pirates who had plagued Roman commerce for the better part of a century.

For most of his life, Pompey seemed to be in the right place at the right time. But that luck ran out. At the pinnacle of his power, Pompey made an alliance called the "triumvirate" with Gaius Julius Caesar and Marcus Licinius Crassus Dives, and sealed it by marrying Caesar's daughter Julia. A decade later, after Crassus's death in the east, and Julia's death in childbirth, Pompey allowed himself to be drawn by conservative elements into a confrontation with Caesar, recently returned from conquering Gaul and now the wealthiest and most powerful man in the Mediterranean world.

Pompey, spurred on by senatorial assurances that he was not only Rome's "best man" but also the savior of the Republic and all of its sacred institutions, met Caesar in battle first at Dhyrrachium, then at Pharsalus, in Greece. Losing both battles, he fled to Egypt, where he was murdered on the orders of the king, who hoped to curry favor with Pompey's former father-in-law, the aforementioned wealthiest, most powerful man in the Mediterranean world.

Bad timing.

MORE MARRIAGES THAN MICKEY ROONEY

OK, not really. And ancient Romans had a far more sanguine view of divorce than we moderns tend to. But Pompey was married *five* times! Each marriage seems to have been motivated by his political career (he married into the family of his rival/ally/rival Caesar, for example, and also into that of the dictator Sulla, and finally into the powerful senatorial family of the Metelli). In the end, none of them could help him defeat Caesar on the field of battle.

★35★
MARCUS TULLIUS CICERO
No Fool Like an Old Fool
(106–43 B.C.)

A learned man, my child, a learned man and a lover of his country.
—*Gaius Julius Caesar Octavianus (Augustus)*

Marcus Tullius Cicero (his nickname "Cicero" means "chickpea" in Latin, possibly a reference to his bulbous nose) was the foremost orator and most successful lawyer of his time. A complicated man, he was dedicated to the Republic, yet aware that the Republic's structure was failing under the weight of its territorial ambitions and her expanding military-industrial complex. Cicero frequently hoped for the best for the Republic while at the same time despairing for her future.

Before his death in 43 B.C., Cicero would become fabulously wealthy, possessing one of the finest houses in Rome and some of the loveliest country villas in Italy. To his peril, he consistently underestimated opponents—such as the two members of the second triumvirate that succeeded the murdered Caesar: that playboy Marcus Antonius and Caesar's heir Octavian.

When Caesar's great-nephew and heir Octavian visited to pay his respects, Cicero developed a seemingly warm relationship with this suddenly wealthy and influential young orphan who came to refer to him as "Pater" ("Father") in their discussions. Acting on this, Cicero set Octavian against Antonius, and persuaded the senate to name Octavian a praetor (judge/military commander).

But, Plutarch notes, "Cicero was led on and cheated, an old man by a young man." Cicero failed to see that Octavian was making common cause with Antonius, and had acquiesced to Antonius's insistence that Cicero's name head the list of any political opponents to be killed in the coming purge. In the end, Cicero failed to take into account just how ruthless a twenty-year-old could be. He would not be the last to do so where Octavian was concerned.

When Antonius's killers caught up with Cicero, he bared his neck for them that they might more easily cut his throat (a move ancient gladiators made as a final sign of their courage in the face of impending death). Not a man previously renowned for physical courage, Cicero's last words are reported to have been: "There is nothing proper about what you are doing, soldier, but do try to kill me properly."

The tragedy of Cicero, a calculating political bastard who overplayed his hand one time too many, is also the tragedy of the end of republican Rome.

LITIGIOUS BASTARD

In ancient Rome, any trial lawyer who successfully prosecuted an officeholder for corruption in office was awarded the criminal's political status as a reward for getting rid of an enemy of the Republic. When Cicero successfully prosecuted Gaius Verres on corruption charges, he received Verres's status as a praetor (a combination of a civilian judge and a military commander) as his reward. Not a military man himself, Cicero used his praetorian status, and the perks associated with it, to their fullest extent. These included being able to be heard in a senate debate before anyone without praetorian status. Talk about cutting in line!

★36★
GAIUS (LICINIUS?) VERRES
One Man's Thief Is Another Man's Art Connoisseur
(CA. 114–43 B.C.)

Because all the world knows that Verres is distinguished by nothing except his monstrous offenses and his obscene wealth.
—*Marcus Tullius Cicero, in his oration Against Verres*

Gaius Verres (we think his second name was "Licinius," but aren't sure) was a career Roman politician who embodied everything that was wrong with politics during the late republican period in ancient Rome. Working his way up through the ranks of the Republic's governmental offices to become a praetor (a combination of magistrate and provincial governor), Verres was equal parts art lover and thug.

Verres determined from an early age to do as so many others were doing at the time: use civil service jobs to cash in. His term serving in the provinces under Gnaeus Cornelius Dolabella only reinforced his larcenous inclinations. While working for Dolabella, Verres looted paintings, statues, and golden idols from the temples of subject populations. When Dolabella was eventually prosecuted for extortion, Verres turned states' evidence in exchange for freedom from prosecution himself.

On his return to Rome, Verres laid out a huge bribe in order to grease election officials and win office as a city magistrate in charge of settling civil cases. He quickly made back the bribe he'd laid out and then some from kickbacks he received from the litigants who appeared before him. While in office, he also manipulated inheritance laws so that the judge overseeing property transfers (in other words, him) received a fee right off the top before the inherited property could be passed to a decedent's heirs.

Verres's criminal career culminated with his appointment as provincial governor of Sicily in 73 B.C. Sicily at the time was a wealthy province, a trading crossroads and possessed of rich farms and ranches along the island's massive internal plain.

Verres helped change all that.

***

APPRENTICE BASTARD

Originally a follower of Gaius Marius, Verres, while still a minor government official, stole a bunch of government funds intended for Marius's troops and joined up with Sulla, Marius's opponent, helping bankroll Sulla's bid to triumph in the civil war against the Marians. Once Sulla was firmly ensconced in power, Verres received the plum job of serving as legatus (a combination of tax collector and army general) in the administration of Gnaeus Cornelius Dolabella, governor of the wealthy province of Cilicia (in Armenia). Dolabella later stood trial for extortion related to his time as governor of Macedonia, so Verres learned at the feet of a master!

So rapacious that no amount of treasure could sate him, Verres took his habitual larceny to new heights, crucifying victims who refused to allow him to seize their property and possessions. When one village elder refused to let him strip the local temple, Verres chained him to a bronze statue in the middle of winter, naked. The old man didn't hold out for long.

But Verres finally went too far. After three years in Sicily, Verres returned to Rome and stood trial for bribery and forgery (in addition to everything else, he was notorious for forging works of art and selling them to rich Romans as antiques).

For someone with his connections, this would not have usually been cause for concern: his allies controlled the judicial process, and they were sympathetic to his case (this kind of looting was so common, prosecution for it was practically a rite of passage). But Verres had drawn as the prosecutor in his case the foremost courtroom lawyer of the era: Marcus Tullius Cicero. Cicero systematically demolished Verres's defense (making a name for himself in the process), so much so that Verres accepted exile and fled to Marseille rather than allow the trial to continue. Decades later, he was executed when he wouldn't surrender his entire collection of ill-gotten art to the Second Triumvirate (they were short of money).

Fitting end for a profiteering bastard.

★37★
GAIUS JULIUS CAESAR
The Gold Standard of Bastardry
(CA. 100–44 B.C.)

> I had rather be first in a village than second at Rome.
>
> —*Gaius Julius Caesar*

Gaius Julius Caesar was renowned not just as a general and politician of the Roman Republic but for his clemency. Time and again, Caesar forgave his enemies and allowed them to prosper, as no other Roman strongman before him had done. His magnanimity would eventually cost him his life, victim of assassination by a handful of senators he numbered among his friends, including several former adversaries whom he had pardoned.

Yet this open-handed great man was personally responsible for the deaths of over 1 million people during the Roman campaign to subjugate Gaul (modern France).

Appointed governor of Gallia Narbonensis (modern-day Provence, in southern France) following his term as consul in 59 B.C., Caesar quickly began to take possession of the unconquered territory of central and northern Gaul by playing the independent Gallic tribes against each other. Over the course of the next six years, Caesar received the submission of no less than 800 cities and towns, defeating the Gauls in battle after battle, until he had subjugated Gaul all the way from Narbonensis in the south to the English Channel in the north.

In 52 B.C., Caesar made plans to return to Rome in triumph. He didn't get the chance.

In response to the call of a charismatic young chieftain named Vercingetorix, the Gauls rose up and killed Roman soldiers and citizens—mostly Roman businessmen looking for "opportunity" of the type that had so enriched their countrymen in the "pacification" (read: looting) of Rome's eastern provinces. Caesar went on the offensive, striking deep into the heart of Gaul and driving Vercingetorix and several thousand of his followers behind the walls of the heavily fortified city of Alesia.

Caesar settled in to besiege the city. Vercingetorix settled in to wait out his besiegers, expecting a large Gallic army to move into the area and drive the hated Romans out. When this army, numbering nearly 200,000, appeared, Caesar responded not by breaking camp, but by building a wall around his encampments, and in effect settling in to be besieged himself, even as he continued to besiege Alesia.

Vercingetorix then drove all noncombatants (women, children, and the elderly) out of Alesia, hoping to extend his food supplies. Caesar, showing himself to be a ruthless bastard, refused to allow these thousands of helpless bystanders through his lines or even to take them as slaves. He let all of them die slowly of exposure or starvation within eyesight of their countrymen still in Alesia.

Caesar's legions repelled attack after attack by the Gauls outside his encampment, and eventually broke the resistance of those within the city's walls. When Vercingetorix rode out of the city and threw down his arms at Caesar's feet, the conqueror's famous impulse to extend mercy to a defeated foe deserted him. Vercingetorix was thrown into prison until he was marched through the streets of Rome during Caesar's triumph five years later, then executed.

QUOTABLE BASTARD

Caesar's ambition was hardly a secret, and hardly unique in ancient Rome. But others did note that Caesar was ambitious even by Roman standards. His political rival Marcus Tullius Cicero once famously remarked to him: "Your spirit has never been content within the narrow confines which nature has imposed upon us."

★38★
MARCUS PORCIUS CATO UTICENSIS
The Bastard as Tiresome, Humorless Scold
(95–46 B.C.)

> The conquering cause pleased the gods,
> but the conquered cause pleased Cato.
>
> —*Lucan,* Pharsalia

Look up the word "contrary" in the dictionary, and you're likely to see this guy's picture next to it. Marcus Porcius Cato Uticensis (known to historians as "Cato the Younger" to distinguish him from his famous forbear of the same name) was a stubborn, silver-spoon-sucking son of an old-old old family. Cato the Elder had distinguished himself by acting as Rome's conscience in her decades-long struggle with Carthage (or as a tiresome, moralistic scold, depending on your point of view). The younger Cato grew up intent on "out-Catoing" his ancestor.

In this, he was, by and large, successful. Caesar himself once wondered aloud why someone like Cato, who, never bothering to go abroad to conquer territory or fight to suppress the Republic's enemies, felt entitled to look down his nose in judgment at someone like Caesar.

But Cato seems to have been capable of "out-arroganting" ancient Roman aristocrats! Time and again he would stake out the moral high ground, set himself up as the defender of what was right, and heap scorn on friend and foe alike. And the Romans thanked him for it.

Although this sort of virtue was easy to admire, it was another thing to like it. Cato got a free pass from most ancient historians who didn't know him personally (especially Plutarch) because of their admiration for his unbending adherence to his principles. But their uncritical acceptance of Cato as the arbiter of what was right and proper does nothing to hide the bald fact that Cato frequently set himself up as the moral authority of his country as a political tool to help in his goal of turning back the clock, keeping the common people (especially the urban poor) in their place, without caring about the cost.

In the end, Cato succeeded in manipulating Pompey into turning on Caesar. But no amount of moral fiber nor stubborn willfulness could make Pompey a better general than Caesar, and Cato and the rest of the *optimates* party who supported the "Great" Pompey were beaten along with him.

Even in defeat, Cato proved contrary. Refusing Caesar's generous offer to let him off the hook for opposing him, Cato embraced martyrdom, stabbing himself to death, something he'd been preparing for his whole life, the end of which he used as a final moral statement.

Contrary bastard.

_____ ✍ _____

PROFITEERING BASTARD?

So Hortensius, an old rich guy in his sixties, tried to get Cato to agree to let him marry Cato's daughter so that he could form a strong alliance with Cato's honorable family, and Cato refused. Hortensius, worried about not having an heir, asked Cato to divorce his wife Marcia instead, so that she might then be married to Hortensius and bear him an heir, which Cato did and which Marcia did. After Hortensius died a few years later, Cato took Marcia back into his household. A guy can be a moral force and still come across as a bit of a nut!

★39★
MARCUS JUNIUS BRUTUS
The Noblest Roman Tax Farmer of Them All
(85–42 B.C.)

> Caesar does not prevent me from acting according to the laws, nor will he prevent me.
>
> —*Marcus Junius Brutus*

Everyone knows the story of Marcus Brutus, that "noblest Roman of them all," a man of unquestioned character, who was good friends with Julius Caesar but helped kill him because he loved the Republic more.

This man of unquestioned character, descended from the near-legendary Brutus who'd chased the last king out of Rome 450 years earlier, actually made his money as a loan shark. Working on the island of Cyprus shortly after it transitioned from client kingdom to Roman territory, Brutus extended loans to people desperate for cash—at an interest rate of 48 percent!

Charging interest at this usurious rate was illegal, but Brutus got an exemption (in part because he was screwing the provincials, not Roman citizens). Within a very short time, Brutus had become an extremely wealthy man.

He had need of the money. His father had been executed on Pompey's orders during Sulla's proscriptions, and the family's possessions had been confiscated by the state.

While all proscription executions carried the stink of murder with them, the killing of the elder Marcus Brutus was particularly rank because he was taken out and killed (likely strangled) after he had surrendered himself to

Pompey's backers, as part of a negotiated deal in which his life was to have been spared. Understandably, the younger Brutus did not take this well; yet, when Pompey and Caesar faced off over the question of which political party's senate representatives would run Rome, Caesar's *populares*, or Pompey and the conservative *optimates*, Brutus doesn't seem to have hesitated. He surprised nearly everyone by siding with Pompey. Historians down the ages have hailed this move as a noble act of putting aside personal interests in the name of patriotism, but they're wrong. Brutus wasn't putting aside his personal interests. He was a rich, wealthy, respected member of the aristocracy who sided with other rich, wealthy members of the aristocracy against that ultimate traitor to his class, Gaius Julius Caesar. How is it patriotic to uphold the old order that benefits you most?

On top of that, after Caesar famously pardoned Brutus, Brutus did what? He joined a plot to assassinate the very man to whom he owed his safety and his own recent advancement (he'd been appointed city praetor by Caesar). When Brutus fell on his own sword after losing the battle of Philippi, he did the most patriotic thing he'd ever done.

———————————— ↻ ————————————

BASTARD'S SON?

Brutus's mother, the formidable Servilia Caepoinis, was the longtime mistress of none other than Gaius Julius Caesar. Ancient historians speculated that Caesar was actually the young Brutus's father, but Caesar likely didn't take up with Servilia until after Brutus was born (Caesar was only fifteen at the time). Caesar sure treated him like a son, though. When Brutus sided with the senate and Pompey against him, Caesar insisted that none of his troops were to fight with Brutus if they encountered him on the battlefield, and he later accepted the young man into his circle of intimates with no penalty for having taken sides against him. Think maybe Caesar was trying to score points with his girlfriend's kid?

★40★
GAIUS CASSIUS LONGINUS
"Lean and Hungry" Bastard
(CA. 85–42 B.C.)

> In great attempts it is glorious even to fail.
> —*Gaius Cassius Longinus*

The guy that Shakespeare would describe centuries later as having a "lean and hungry look" knew a thing or two about failure. Between having an older brother whose track record of corruption kept him from getting elected consul, and his own adventures during Crassus's disastrous campaign against the Parthians in 53 B.C., Cassius had witnessed failure on an epic scale by the time he became a leading opponent of Julius Caesar.

And yet, just like the Bard wrote, Cassius was in many ways the spirit behind the conspiracy to kill Caesar. Never mind that the ever-magnanimous Caesar had pardoned Cassius for backing Caesar's rival Pompey. In fact, owing his life to Caesar seems to have sharpened Cassius's resolve to see him sacrificed on the altar of republican values.

When Caesar began selecting men of ability for various praetorships (magistracies) throughout the Republic's territories, including the coveted city praetorship of Rome itself, Cassius, eminently qualified for this position, found himself in competition with his brother-in-law, Marcus Brutus, for it. Caesar conceded that Cassius was the more qualified, but either because of outright favoritism or because he had reason to distrust Cassius, Caesar choose Brutus for the position. It was at this point that Cassius began plotting against Caesar.

This made him a hypocrite, because while he claimed to his co-conspirators to be protecting the Republic, his actual reason for plotting against Caesar was malice.

Somehow Cassius managed to pull it off; he succeeded in inveigling the more highly regarded Brutus into his plot, attaching Brutus's name (and consequently the names of a whole bunch of people with better reputations than Cassius's own) to it. After they had killed Caesar, it was Brutus who insisted that the life of Marcus Antonius be spared—Cassius wanted the playboy dead, saying that Brutus had underestimated him.

As it turned out, Cassius was right.

What followed were two years of jockeying for power between Antonius and Caesar's heir Octavian and their adherents on one side, and Brutus, Cassius, and the other conspirators (and their followers) on the other. It all came to a head at the battle of Philippi in Greece in late 42 B.C. Brutus succeeded in defeating Octavian's troops and forcing his retreat, but Cassius lost in a separate engagement to the hated Antonius. Determined not to be taken alive, Cassius committed suicide with the help of a devoted freedman, Pindarus. Brutus would soon follow him in death, and with them went the Republic for which they'd killed Caesar.

⁂

BASTARD-IN-LAW

Cassius was the half-brother of Marcus Brutus's wife, making Brutus Cassius's brother-in-law. And according to the biographer Plutarch, Cassius suffered by the inevitable comparison. Caesar's supporters, Plutarch wrote, "laid whatever was barbarous and cruel [about the conspiracy to kill Caesar] to the charge of Cassius," who was "not [Brutus's] equal in honesty and pureness of purpose."

MARCUS ANTONIUS
Dandy, Playboy, Ruthless Bastard
(CA. 86–30 B.C.)

> He was too lazy to pay attention to the complaints of persons
> who were injured; he listened impatiently to petitions; and he
> had an ill name for familiarity with other people's wives.
> —*Plutarch*, Life of Antony

The image of Marcus Antonius (also known as "Marc Antony") that has come down to us through the ages is a complicated one. By turns industrious and lazy, open-handed and murderous, Antonius had a reputation as both a maker of trouble and a maker of deals. In the end, neither his considerable talents nor his equally considerable faults made much difference. He crossed the buzz saw that was Octavian, and paid for it.

Born into a well-connected family, Antonius was a distant cousin of the strongman Gaius Julius Caesar. His grandfather was a great orator who was killed during Marius's and Cinna's proscriptions. His father was an undistinguished public official who died while Antonius was young. His mother remarried, this time to Publius Cornelius Lentulus, a politician who was eventually executed for his part in Catiline's conspiracy (an act for which Antonius never forgave Cicero, the consul who exposed Catiline's plot and saw to it that the ringleaders were put to death).

Antonius quickly developed a reputation as a good soldier and a careless administrator, a spendthrift who was 5 million dollars (in today's money) in debt before he turned twenty-five, and a good-time party boy who was great at taking orders (especially Caesar's). Little wonder that so many of his opponents underestimated him.

After Caesar was murdered, Antonius spent the next fourteen years alternately at odds and allied with Caesar's heir, Octavian. Eventually they agreed to an alliance wherein they split the Roman world between them and sealed the bargain with Antonius's marriage to Octavian's sister, Octavia. The two were soon at odds again, when Antonius threw over his wife for a very public affair with Cleopatra, Queen of Egypt.

The outcome shouldn't really have been in doubt. Antonius pretty much lost his head over his new girlfriend (who had been Caesar's before him—Antonius always wanted to be Caesar), at her urging deeding their children huge territories carved out of Roman conquests in the eastern Mediterranean. The result was outrage in Rome and a climactic naval battle at Actium in 31 B.C. between Cleopatra's fleet and Octavian's navy. Within a matter of weeks, both Antonius and Cleopatra had committed suicide.

And those children that Antonius tried to provide for? They were sent to Rome, where Antonius's widow Octavia (he had never bothered to divorce her) raised them as her own.

A BASTARD THREESOME

According to contemporary accounts, Antonius screwed his way through half the available women in Rome, and frequently didn't stop at women. One of Antonius's boyfriends was a guy named Gaius Scribonius Curio, whom he'd known and partied with since his teen years. When Curio died, Antonius almost immediately married his widow, Fulvia, who bore him a son. Theirs was more than just a political alliance (although it was clearly that as well), and although Antonius was never faithful to Fulvia, they were clearly devoted to each other. The historian Cassius Dio reports that when Antonius managed to get his lifelong enemy Cicero executed, Fulvia had the great orator's severed head brought to her so she could stab that previously eloquent tongue with her knitting needles!

★42★
GAIUS JULIUS CAESAR OCTAVIANUS AUGUSTUS
Sage Old Bastard Who Died in Bed, Redux
(63 B.C.–A.D. 14)

> You, boy, owe everything to your name.
> —*Marcus Antonius to Octavian*, 43 B.C.

If ever a man was both right and wrong at the same time, it was Marcus Antonius when he made the above statement. While it was true that Octavian, then barely out of his teens, was rich because he was the adopted son and heir of Gaius Julius Caesar, what Antonius failed to comprehend was that Octavian possessed reserves of both guile and resolve that Antonius at his dilettante best could not possibly hope to match. Their relationship, begun in barely tolerated loathing wedded to mutual self-interest, culminated in Antonius's downfall and death in 30 B.C. and Octavian's consolidation of power in the Mediterranean world as the first emperor of Rome.

Octavian's father died when he was little, and after his mother's remarriage she and his stepfather paid little attention to the boy. His great-uncle Gaius Julius Caesar took an interest in both his upbringing and his education. Every bit as shrewd as his illustrious relative, Octavian was possessed of a far less forgiving nature. Caesar was famous for his willingness to forgive and pardon his enemies. Not so Octavian.

During his lifetime, he exiled his only child, his daughter Julia, on charges of treason and adultery (by all reports, of the two she is certain to have committed the adultery, many, many times). During the bloody proscriptions that followed Caesar's murder, the young Octavian, who had developed a relationship with fellow bastard Cicero so warm that he called the older man "father," agreed with Marcus Antonius that Cicero must be killed. After the defeat and suicides of Antonius and Cleopatra, Octavian's forces took over Egypt, and when Cleopatra's children fell into his power, he had his own cousin (Julius Caesar's son Caesarion) killed, although the boy was only sixteen. He did the same with Antonius's eldest son (and heir), seventeen-year-old Antyllus, brutally beheading him in front of his legions.

WHAT'S IN A BASTARD'S NAME?

Born Gaius Octavius Thurinus in 63 B.C. the boy was named after his most esteemed relative: Caesar, his grandmother's brother. When Caesar adopted him, his name became Gaius Julius Caesar Octavianus. He preferred to be called "Caesar" after that point, not just because it was a powerful political reminder of his connection to his great-uncle, but because he barely knew his own father and heartily disliked his stepfather. After he had held supreme power for decades, the senate voted him the title (not name) Augustus, which in Latin means "honored," or "revered." We get our word "august" from it. The senate also renamed the month of Sextilis in the old Roman calendar "August" after him.

Although during his long life and political career he cultivated a public image of a modest man, uninterested in holding power himself except as it was delegated to him by the senate, Octavian proved a most ruthless man: taking on the Roman state and using his personal popularity, the enormous wealth his great-uncle had left him in his will, and his considerable political skills to convert the anarchic late Republic into a smooth running dictatorship called "the Principate." During this entire time, Octavian never allowed himself to be referred to in public as anything other than "Caesar," claiming he was nothing more than a sort of "First Among Citizens," doing his duty to his country.

In reality, Octavian controlled the levers of power in the Roman state until he died in his bed at age seventy-six. This was the man who was fond of boasting: "I found Rome brick and left her marble," speaking of his building programs. But what he really did was find Rome chaotic and leave her orderly.

A task that requires a wide streak of bastardry!

★43★
LIVIA DRUSILLA
Stage Mother for an Empire
(58 B.C.— A.D. 29)

In domestic virtue she was of the old school, though her affability went further than was approved by women of the elder world. An imperious mother, she was an accommodating wife, and an excellent match for the subtleties of her husband and the insincerity of her son.

—*Tacitus*, The Annals

Livia Drusilla, the wife of Rome's first emperor, fellow bastard Gaius Julius Caesar Octavianus (Augustus), comes down to us through the millennia as an opaque figure at best. Every bit as capable of playing a role with all the sincerity of her nearly matchless husband, Livia made a point of playing the doting wife and caring mother in public, embracing the traditional role of the virtuous Roman matron, consumed with hearth and home, leaving business and politics to "her men."

In reality, she was a political player and behind-the-scenes power broker, one of only two people her husband seems to have trusted during his entire long life (the other being his lifelong friend and son-in-law, Marcus Agrippa). Livia made use of that trust to influence the emperor (and others) in favor of her sons: the scholarly, moody military man Tiberius and his younger brother, the brilliant, likeable Drusus.

The accusations of several ancient historians that Livia poisoned those who stood in the way of her own sons are probably just so much axe-grinding. That said, she clearly influenced her husband, and no doubt pushed him in his choice of Tiberius as his eventual heir.

That is not to say that her hands were clean of all wrongdoing.

Once Octavian (by then called Augustus) was dead, Livia covered up the news of his death, issuing proclamations in his name and sealing up the house where he'd died so that no one got in or out without her consent. This gave Tiberius time to get to Augustus's bedside, and by extension, to consolidate his power. It is probable that Livia ordered the murder of Augustus's only living grandson, Agrippa Postumus, without Tiberius's consent.

While Livia lived to see her son succeed her husband as emperor, it's anybody's guess how much she actually enjoyed his reign. Tiberius avoided seeing or communicating with his mother at all costs pretty much for the rest of her life. When she died in A.D. 29, a very old woman of eighty-six, he skipped her funeral and refused to honor the provisions of her will.

——————————————— ✍ ———————————————

COLD-BLOODED MAMA BASTARD

Roman aristocrats could be a cold-blooded lot, and frequently had completely unsentimental attitudes toward divorce. One person might marry and divorce several times over, with these marriages largely seen as property matters, rather than love matches. Livia seems to have been involved in relationships for both sentimental and unsentimental reasons. She hitched her wagon to Octavian's star when she was still in her teens, beginning an affair with him while she was still married to her first husband (and pregnant with their second child, Drusus). She divorced said husband (a much older man who was on the wrong side of the political conflict between Octavian and the murderers of Julius Caesar) while still pregnant with Drusus. And she quickly married Octavian, again while still pregnant with the same baby!

★44★
TIBERIUS CAESAR AUGUSTUS
Bastard as the Grumpy Old Man Who Lives on Your Street
(42 B.C.– A.D. 37)

[Tiberius] ordered the death of all who were lying in prison under accusation of complicity with Sejanus. There lay, singly or in heaps, the unnumbered dead, of every age and sex, the illustrious with the obscure. . . . The force of terror had utterly extinguished the sense of human fellowship, and with the growth of cruelty, pity was thrust aside.

—*Tacitus*, The Annals

Rome's second emperor was a reluctant bastard if ever there was one. A proven military man and philosopher who vastly preferred books to politics, Tiberius succeeded his stepfather Augustus (Octavian) pretty much because he was the only heir left standing when Augustus died in A.D. 14, after more than fifty years of running the Roman state.

By the time the throne was thrust upon him by Augustus's death, Tiberius seems to have resigned himself to the job, and for a while proved an able, if unspectacular, ruler. But he was in his mid-fifties by the time he became emperor, and never possessed the common touch; the Roman people didn't much like him, and he seems to have reciprocated that lack of affection. He relied more and more on his right-hand man, the praetorian prefect Sejanus—a bastard with ideas of his own when it came to the imperial throne.

In A.D. 31, Tiberius got wind of Sejanus's plotting to take the throne from him. He tricked his unsuspecting praetorian prefect into coming to the Senate House without his usual praetorian escort, then had him seized and executed. But Tiberius didn't stop there: he began a bloody purge of not just Sejanus's followers, but of every member of his family and all of his friends—basically everyone who knew him. Tiberius even had his own daughter-in-law killed when it was revealed that she had helped Sejanus poison her husband years earlier.

In the end, though, he was only forestalling the inevitable. On his death-bed, when the seventy-seven-year-old emperor rallied and asked for some-thing to eat, Sejanus's successor (and executioner) Macro took a pillow and smothered the old man to make way for his young heir, that nutty bastard Caligula.

MAMA'S BASTARD

The ultimate stage mother, Tiberius's mother Livia spared no effort manipulating her husband (Tiberius's stepfather Augustus) into favoring her sons by her first marriage in his succession plans, since Augustus had no sons of his own. Rumor had it that when Augustus finally kicked off himself, it was because Livia had poisoned him to get him out of the way before he changed his mind about handing off his position and his vast fortune to his gloomy stepson!

★45★
LUCIUS AELIUS
SEJANUS
Clearing the Way for a Monster
(20 B.C.–A.D. 31)

A blend of arrogance and servility, [Sejanus] concealed behind a carefully modest exterior an unbounded lust for power. Sometimes this impelled him to lavish excesses, but more often to incessant work. And that is as damaging as excess when the throne is its aim.

—*Tacitus*, The Annals of Imperial Rome

Shades of *The Godfather*! Great man conflicted about ruling a powerful family enterprise, weighed down in his old age by the assorted stresses of running said enterprise. Along comes a powerful, charismatic, innovative younger guy, ambitious, not afraid to make himself useful, all the while plotting his own eventual takeover.

That's the story of the Roman emperor Tiberius and the helpful younger man angling to be his heir-apparent, Lucius Aelius Sejanus.

Sejanus seduced the wife of Tiberius's son and heir, used her to help get that son and heir out of the way, got himself betrothed to his mistress once she became the dead son's widow, and for several years was de facto ruler of the Roman Empire.

The historian Tacitus writes that Sejanus, a commoner, nursed a private ambition to become emperor once he'd been made praetorian prefect in A.D. 14, but "Sejanus' ambitions were impeded by the well-stocked imperial house, including a son and heir—in his prime—and grown-up grandchildren." So Sejanus set about knocking off these heirs, starting with Tiberius's grown son-and-heir-to-the-throne, Drusus. This he accomplished by seducing Drusus's none-too-bright wife, then getting her to help him poison her husband. When Drusus died of a sudden "illness" in A.D. 23, no one seems to have suspected a thing.

Sejanus became de facto ruler of the Roman Empire, running things in the name of Tiberius. He slowly got other heirs out of the way. In A.D. 29, Agrippina, widow of Tiberius's nephew Germanicus, and her sons Drusus (yes, yet another Drusus) and Nero (no, not that Nero) were sent into exile on charges made by Sejanus that they were plotting against Tiberius. Agrippina wound up starving herself to death, whereas Drusus was forced to commit suicide. Nero's end was particularly gruesome. Starved to death himself, he was apparently at one point so crazed with hunger that he attempted to eat his own mattress!

In the end, all of Sejanus's plotting came to naught, because Tiberius's aunt Antonia sent the emperor a letter accusing Sejanus of attempting to usurp the throne. With that single string pulled, the entire carefully constructed plot began to unravel. Sejanus was taken by surprise in the Senate House, arrested, condemned, and in short order strangled, then had his corpse thrown down the Gemonian Steps, where an angry mob tore it to pieces.

The major unintended consequence of Sejanus's plot was that by getting rid of Drusus and Nero, he, more than any other individual, was responsible for clearing the way for their younger brother, that nutty bastard Caligula, to succeed Tiberius as emperor.

BASTARD MENTOR/MENTEE

Tiberius, who had stayed alive and grown old in the imperial succession in part because he trusted no one, was by all accounts completely taken in by Sejanus, at one point describing him to the senate as "the partner of my labors."

★46★
CALIGULA
You Call That Nag a Roman Consul?
(A.D. 12–41)

> The method of execution [Caligula] preferred was to inflict
> numerous small wounds; and his familiar order: 'Make him feel
> that he is dying!' soon became proverbial.
> —*Suetonius, gossipy Roman historian*

These days, Roman-emperor-as-lunatic seems nothing short of a cliché. Colorful examples of this archetype include Nero (who fancied himself an athlete and entertainer), Commodus (who walked around dressed up like Hercules), and Elagabalus (a cross-dresser who "married" one of his slave charioteers).

But the granddaddy of them all, the one who originated the whole "mad emperor" meme, was a man who married his second wife by interrupting her marriage to another man and stepping into the bridegroom's place, who insisted on being worshipped as a god while still alive, who threatened to make his favorite racehorse by turns either a senator or a consul, and who collected seashells along the coast of the English Channel as a symbol of his "great victory" over the sea god Neptune!

Ladies and gentlemen, meet Rome's third emperor, Gaius, better known these days as Caligula.

While there's no question that Caligula was one of Rome's most unforgettable bastards, it's tough to say for sure whether he was out-and-out crazy, or just a really vindictive bastard with a warped sense of humor, twisted by the difficult years that preceded his taking the throne at age twenty-five.

His father died when he was only seven. His mother (a vicious harpy known as Agrippina) and two of his elder brothers were executed on Tiberius's orders when Caligula was still in his teens. Following these executions,

Caligula began to blatantly suck up to his great-uncle, so impressing the old goat with his apparent indifference to the deaths of those closest to him that Tiberius made Caligula his heir, joking on more than one occasion that he "was rearing a viper for the Roman people."

His words turned out to be prophetic.

After a promising start on his ascension to the throne in A.D. 41, Caligula was struck by a strange illness that nearly killed him. He was never the same after that, behaving in an increasingly odd manner, especially with his three younger sisters (with whom he was later alleged to have committed incest). When his favorite sister Drusilla died suddenly, Caligula was beside himself with grief. Tongues began to wag.

The emperor responded to this gossip by becoming ever more bloodthirsty. Sensitive about his premature baldness, he was known on several occasions to order the executions of anyone mentioning his hair, or even of standing anywhere above him, where they might actually be able to see his solar sex panel for themselves.

Coupled with his insistence that he was a god, and ought to be addressed as such, and that he and the moon were siblings, his lavish spending, and the ever-more-bloodthirsty manner in which he suppressed real and imagined plots against his life, it's small wonder that someone eventually succeeded in killing the bastard in A.D. 41. He was not yet thirty years old.

A BASTARD BY ANY NICKNAME

The word "Caligula" in Latin means "Little Boots." Gaius earned this nickname living in a frontier army camp with his father, a popular general named Germanicus. While still a small boy, the future emperor wore miniature versions of the standard-issue hobnailed, open-toed boots (not your ordinary sandals!) worn by Roman infantry. This type of boot was called a caliga; hence the little boy's nickname.

> No suspicion was too trivial, nor the inspirer of it too insignificant, to drive [Claudius] on to precaution and vengeance, once a slight uneasiness entered his mind. One of two parties to a suit, when he made his morning call, took Claudius aside, and said that he had dreamed that he was murdered by someone; then a little later pretending to recognize the assassin, he pointed out his opponent.... The latter was immediately seized, as if caught red-handed, and hurried off to execution.
> —*Suetonius,* The Life of Claudius

Dismissed early on as a stammering boob with the intellect of a potted plant, the Roman emperor Claudius had the last laugh on those who overlooked him while killing off most of his adult male relatives. When his nephew Caligula was murdered in A.D. 41, the same guards who had killed him put Claudius on the throne.

What these praetorians got for their trouble was a straight-up bribe: 15,000 sesterces (small silver pieces) per man. What the Roman people got for theirs was rather more a mixed bag.

Claudius demonstrated surprising ability and shrewdness when it came to administering his empire, and under him Roman troops finally conquered part of the island of Britain (something his ancestor Julius Caesar had attempted, but had never been able to accomplish). This was due in large part to his trusting in imperial freedmen to run his empire for him.

Having witnessed political murder after political murder during his lifetime, Claudius was terrified of being assassinated. And not without reason: within a year of his taking the throne, one of his provincial governors rebelled against him (the rebellion was stamped out within a week). His first wife, Messalina, attempted a palace coup while he was out of Rome on religious business, conducting a sham marriage with a lover. He flew into a rage (he possessed a terrible temper) and had them both seized and executed.

In the end, Claudius's fear of assassination proved prophetic. The emperor who once drunkenly remarked that "it was his destiny first to suffer and finally to punish the infamy of his wives" was undone by his own terrible taste in women. He replaced the slutty and manipulative Messalina with his own niece, the equally slutty and manipulative Agrippina, who, in order to see her own son Nero made emperor, poisoned Claudius in A.D. 54.

SHAKY, DROOLING DULLARD AND SNOT-NOSED BASTARD

Claudius's own mother referred to him as "a monster of a man, not finished but merely begun by Dame Nature." According to the Roman biographer Suetonius, if she wanted to insult anyone's intelligence, she would call the object of her contempt "a bigger fool than her son Claudius." The future emperor suffered from an unknown childhood illness that left him with a pronounced limp. As if this weren't enough, Suetonius tells us that Claudius "had many disagreeable traits . . . he would foam at the mouth and trickle at the nose; he stammered besides and his head was very shaky at times."

★48★
NERO
Actor, Singer, Poet, Athlete, Matricidal Mamma's Boy
(A.D. 37–68)

Nero substituted as culprits, and punished with the utmost refinements of cruelty, a class of men, loathed for their vices, whom the crowd styled Christians. . . . And derision accompanied their end: they were covered with wild beasts' skins and torn to death by dogs; or they were fastened on crosses, and when daylight failed were burned to serve as lamps by night.
—*Tacitus*, The Annals of Imperial Rome

Humanist, patron of the arts, actor, singer, poet, playwright, and athlete. That is how the Roman emperor Nero Claudius Caesar Augustus Germanicus wished to be remembered. But he's mostly remembered for fiddling while Rome burned.

He was first a political pawn of others (especially his monstrous mother), then an upstart who had said domineering mother murdered, and later an emperor who initiated the persecution of Christians (supposedly to cover up his own guilt in starting the enormous fire that gutted Rome in A.D. 64).

Nero was related to the line of emperors descended from Julius Caesar through his mother, Agrippina. One of the most ambitious and notorious stage mothers in history, Agrippina connived to marry her uncle, the reigning emperor Claudius (that dynastic inbreeding stuff again) in order to get Nero, her child by a previous marriage, in line for the throne.

Guided by such heavyweights as the Roman philosopher and playwright Seneca, Nero began his reign on a mostly positive note, in spite of his mother

Agrippina's seemingly insatiable lust for power. When he'd had enough of her trying to rule through him, Nero concocted a scheme wherein the boat in which she was travelling literally fell apart around her. When Agrippina proved more formidable than the sea, managing to reach the shore and from there her villa, Nero sent trusted soldiers to murder her in her bed. Her reported last words were "Strike here! This bore Nero!" while pointing at her womb.

―――――――――――――   ✑   ―――――――――――――

FIDDLING BASTARD

Everyone knows the story of how Nero fiddled while Rome burned. The germ of that story (and the notion that the emperor used Christians as scapegoats for the great fire that engulfed Rome in A.D. 64) comes from the Roman historian Tacitus: "For a rumor had spread that, while the city was burning, Nero had gone on his private stage and, comparing modern calamities with ancient, had sung the destruction of Troy." To make matters worse, Nero seized a large chunk of the burned-out center of the city, where he erected a huge statute of himself as well as a sprawling, lavish new imperial residence dubbed the Domus Aureum ("Golden House"). When it was completed, Nero is said to have toured it, remarking, "At last a house fit for a human being to live in!" What he thought of those whom he'd dispossessed in order to build his golden house is not recorded.

From that point onward, there was no stopping the guy. As noted, Nero fancied himself quite the artist (reportedly saying, "What an artist dies with me!" on his deathbed). He acted on the stage, wrote and performed his own plays (a move that scandalized an ever-more-disenchanted Roman populace), and gave concerts wherein he played the lyre and sang. And heaven help you if you tried to leave one of these concerts early: several men who did were cut down by the Praetorian Guard for leaving the emperor's presence without permission. Pregnant women were reported to have gone into labor and given birth during Nero's performances!

Nero even competed in the Olympic Games, where (surprise, surprise) he won every single event in which he participated.

By A.D. 68, the most important of the emperor's supporters, the army, had had enough. Several legions rose in revolt, with one of them proclaiming their general (Galba) emperor. Historians maintain that had Nero actually gone out and conquered some new province or fought an invading enemy with his legions, his eccentricities might have been overlooked. As it was, he cut his own throat in order to avoid capture by Galba's soldiers.

Bastard.

★49★
SERVIUS SULPICIUS GALBA
How Being Too Cheap to Pay Off Your Promised Bribes Can Be a Bad Idea
(3 B.C.– A.D. 68)

> [Galba] seemed too great to be a subject so long as he remained a subject, and by general consent, he would have been a capable ruler, had he not ruled.
> —*Tacitus*, The Histories

Servius Sulpicius Galba was born in 3 B.C. to a wealthy northern Italian family. Over the course of his life, he held a variety of military and government positions, earning a reputation for bravery and competency as both a military commander and as a civil servant. He was also cheap, short-sighted, inflexible, and a terrible judge of character. Unfortunately, these less-than-sterling character traits did not reveal themselves until after Galba became emperor. By that time, it was far too late for him to save himself from a violent end.

When Galba was governor of a province in Spain, a complicated series of events resulted in the Praetorian Guard deposing Nero (causing Nero's suicide) and in Galba's allies in Rome (many of them senators) seizing an opportunity.

They bribed the praetorians to accept Galba as emperor.

Once installed as emperor, Galba set about establishing and stabilizing his regime by trying to balance the imperial budget. For the previous thirteen years, Nero had spent lavishly on foolish projects, showering his favorites with largesse, and allowing his imperial freedmen (ex-slaves working as civil servants) to embezzle large sums of money. The predict-able result was that Galba found himself saddled with a crushing debt.

Most of the measures Galba took did not go over well with the citizens (government takeaways rarely do). For example, the new emperor decreed that every cash giveaway Nero had made (and there were thousands on record) would need to be repaid to the tune of 90 percent. The grumbling began.

At the best of times, put forward by the most virtuous and honest of gov-ernments, this sort of decision would have been unpopular. But the govern-ment that implemented it was neither of these things. Once Galba assumed the imperial purple, all of those unscrupulous folks who had helped him expected to get a little piece of the action. They were not disappointed. Galba's civil servants were, if anything, greedier and more open about their plundering the empire's taxes reserves than Nero's had been. One of Galba's boyfriends (see sidebar) named Icelus is reputed to have pocketed more in a few months than Nero's gang had managed to steal over the course of his entire reign!

When Galba tried to welsh on his deal with the praetorians and not pay them the cash bounty they had been promised, it was the last straw. Legions on the Rhine frontier mutinied. There was panic on the streets of Rome. When Galba went to the Forum to face down his opponents, he was thrown from his litter and stabbed to death.

GAY BASTARD

Although ancient history is rife with stories of "great men" who had both female and male lovers, Galba was, according to that Mr. Blackwell of ancient Rome, Suetonius, unique among Rome's early emperors in preferring men to women: "In sexual matters he was more inclined to males, and then none but the hard bodied and those past their prime."

★50★
MARCUS SALVIUS OTHO
The Emperor as Scheming Pretty Boy
(A.D. 32–69)

> When civil war in the balance lay, and mincing Otho might have
> won the day, bloodshed too costly did he spare the land, and
> pierced his heart with an unfaltering hand.
>
> —*Martial*, Epigrams

One of Nero's closest friends and confidants during the early years of his reign was a fashion-plate dilettante named Marcus Salvius Otho (the two men were rumored to have been lovers). Vain, shallow, and frivolous, Otho only survived Nero's fall because he and the emperor argued over a woman (?!?). By A.D. 68, Otho found himself posted as governor of a frontier province in what is now Portugal, far from Rome and from the bloodbath that followed Nero's death.

An early supporter of Galba's coup, Otho expected to be selected as the elderly new emperor's heir apparent. The fly in the ointment for the ambitious young man was the fact that Otho's family were commoners, without the distinguished pedigree that Galba was seeking in a successor (in hopes of shoring up his regime while it was still in its infancy and thus vulnerable), so he was passed over for a rival whom Galba adopted as both his son and heir.

But Galba had recently committed an inexcusable blunder: he had stiffed Rome's city police force (and the emperor's personal bodyguard), the Praetorian Guard, out of the large cash bribe they'd been offered to pave the way for his march on Rome.

Seeing his chance, the wealthy Otho slipped into the praetorian camp and offered them a bribe of his own. Unlike Galba, he made good on his promise. The praetorians declared Otho emperor, and Galba was murdered in the Forum during the resulting riots.

As this was happening, one of the legions on the Rhine frontier mutinied and declared its general (a fat nobody named Vitellius) emperor. Vitellius's legion marched on Rome. Otho sent his troops out to face them at the Po River in northern Italy. Vitellius's forces won the resulting battle (the Battle of Bedriacum), routing Otho's army and sending them reeling back to their master in Rome.

At this point, Otho either lost his nerve or developed a conscience. When news of the disaster reached him, the emperor sent his family word that they ought to do whatever it took to save themselves. The Roman historian Cassius Dio records a pretty speech (likely fabricated) that Otho made to his troops, deploring the possibility of civil war and determining to sacrifice himself rather than Roman soldiers to fight each other in his name.

Then he went to bed, only to rise the next morning and commit suicide by stabbing himself to death.

$\backsim$

FOPPISH BASTARD

Otho was notorious for going to great lengths where his appearance was concerned. As the gossipy Roman historian Suetonius tells us: "He had the hair of his body plucked out, and because of the thinness of his locks wore a wig. . . . Moreover, they say that he used to shave every day and smear his face with moist bread . . . so as never to have a beard."

★51★
AULUS VITELLIUS
The Fat Bastard Who Tried to Sell His Throne
(A.D. 12–69)

Seldom has the support of the army been gained by any man through honorable means to the degree that [Vitellius] won it through worthlessness.
—*Tacitus, The Histories*

Historians refer to the twelve months after the death of the emperor Nero as the "Year of four emperors," because in the civil war that followed, several different claimants came forward to take the imperial throne.

The third of these emperors was arguably the least ambitious of the bunch, a notorious glutton and decades-long hanger-on at the imperial court who managed to flatter his way into a variety of lucrative political jobs serving under three different emperors. This was Aulus Vitellius, who had the misfortune to command a legion whose discipline crumbled away shortly after his greatest victory, largely because of his own bad decisions.

It can truthfully be said of Vitellius that it wasn't his idea to become emperor. His troops started the whole thing by refusing to swear allegiance to the new emperor Galba and proclaiming Vitellius emperor. Two of his subordinates, the generals Fabius Valens and Aulus Caecina Alienus, sealed the deal by leading his advance guard into Italy.

It was Valens and Caecina who defeated the troops of the new emperor Otho at the Battle of Bedriacum. All Vitellius had to do was follow along as they made their way to Rome. Once there, Vitellius got himself proclaimed emperor by the senate, but the tide had already turned. Several legions along the northern and eastern frontiers declared for the general Vespasian, and he in his turn marched on Rome.

Before Vespasian got to Italy, Vitellius, like Otho before him, lost his nerve. He approached Vespasian's older brother, Flavius Sabinus, one of the consuls for that year, who was barricaded along with a number of other of Vespasian's supporters on the Capitoline Hill in Rome, and made a deal to surrender the throne to Vespasian, all in the name of peace (and a huge bribe). But the deal fell through because Vitellius's Praetorian Guard wouldn't allow him to follow through with his resignation, instead pushing him to turn on Sabinus, which he promptly did, ordering the temple where Sabinus and his followers had taken refuge burned down around their ears.

The move sealed Vitellius's fate. When Vespasian's soldiers came looking for him not long afterward, he was hiding in his gatekeeper's quarters.

By that point it didn't matter that none of it, from proclaiming himself emperor to betraying and killing the well-respected brother of one of his rivals, had been his idea. Vitellius paid the ultimate penalty: as Suetonius tells us, he was bound and dragged through the streets of Rome to the Gemonian Steps, where criminals were executed. There he was tortured and beheaded, with his headless body tossed into the Tiber.

FAT, GIMPY BASTARD WITH A GIN BLOSSOM NOSE

Vitellius had a very distinctive appearance. According to the Roman biographer Suetonius, "He was in fact abnormally tall, with a face usually flushed from hard drinking, a huge belly, and one thigh crippled from being struck once upon a time by a four-horse chariot, when he was in attendance on Gaius as he was driving."

★52★
DOMITIAN
No Bald Jokes!
(?-84 B.C.)

> Under Domitian more than half our wretchedness consisted of
> watching and being watched, while our very sighs were scored
> against us, and the blanched faces of us all were revealed in
> deadly contrast to that one scowling blush behind which Domi-
> tian sheltered against all shame.
>
> —*Tactius*, Agricola

Talk about your tough acts to follow. First, there was the no-nonsense military hero emperor, hard-headed and the favorite of his legions, founder of
his dynasty (Vespasian, founder of the Flavians). Then there was his elder
son, also a skilled military man, very popular, and trained by his illustrious
father to succeed him in the toughest job in the ancient world, only to die
young from a mysterious illness (Titus). Who in their right mind wants to
be the guy who comes along next in this progression? It sure wasn't Titus
Flavius Domitianus, the Roman emperor better known as Domitian.

Even so, Domitian proved himself talented in many ways. He was good
with money, and added to the empire's infrastructure (roads, public buildings, frontier fortresses).

But he inherited a bankrupt treasury upon taking the throne in A.D. 81.
He responded by condemning wealthy citizens on trumped-up charges and
either executing or banishing them, then confiscating their property.

But more than that, Domitian just wasn't a very happy guy. According
to the Roman biographer Suetonius, who grew up during Domitian's reign,
the emperor "used to say that the lot of princes was most unhappy, since

when they had discovered a conspiracy, no one believed them unless they had been killed."

Over the years, this unease and suspicion of those around him metastasized into full-on paranoia. By A.D. 93, Domitian had begun his "reign of terror," according to the Roman historian Tacitus, a senator during this time. Dozens of prominent citizens (many of them senators) wound up proscribed and dead.

The philosopher Pliny the Younger, who entered the senate late in Domitian's reign, wrote of the experience in a letter to a friend, calling it "a time when seven of my friends had been put to death or banished . . . so that I stood amidst the flames of thunderbolts dropping all around me, and there were certain clear indications to make me suppose a like end was awaiting me."

Domitian's paranoia became, as with so many other tyrants, a self-fulfilling prophecy. The plot he had feared during his entire adult life came to pass in early A.D. 96.

The previous year Domitian had exiled his niece and executed her husband (for treason, of course). The niece's steward, a fellow named Stephanus, stayed on in the emperor's service and conspired with Domitian's own chamberlain Parthenius and several others to do the despot in.

They caught the emperor preparing to take an afternoon nap without a weapon handy, and Stephanus stabbed him. The other conspirators rushed in, and Domitian was dead, aged fifty-years and having ruled for fifteen.

––––––––––––––––––   ✒   ––––––––––––––––––

BALDING BASTARD
Another one of those balding emperors sensitive about his thinning hair, Domitian disguised his condition with wigs and laurel wreaths, and actually wrote a book about hair care.

★53★
COMMODUS
The Emperor as Hercules
(A.D. 161–192)

> More savage than Domitian, more foul than Nero. As he did unto others, let it be done unto him.
> —*Referendum of the Roman senate on the death of Commodus*

With so many whack jobs populating the ranks of the emperors of Rome, an imperial bastard has to really excel to make the cut for this book. In the case of Aurelius Commodus Antoninus Augustus, we get a doozy: a guy who convinced himself that he was the reincarnation of the god Hercules, competed in the arena as a gladiator, renamed all the months in the calendar (and eventually the city of Rome) after himself, and died the victim of a plot spearheaded by his own mistress!

Never one to take responsibility when he could get someone else to do the hard work, on inheriting the imperial throne from his father Marcus Aurelius in A.D. 180, Commodus immediately began to delegate authority to a series of hand-picked subordinates.

Within two years, Commodus's own sister led a conspiracy against him, and it very nearly resulted in his death. Badly spooked by this attempt, the emperor all but ceased appearing in public during the next couple of years, allowing persuasive subordinates to rule in his name (several of whom were, in their turn, assassinated). The end result was that the son of one of the empire's most able rulers and its greatest philosopher became the figurehead of a vast police state.

And what a figurehead he was! Tall, handsome, muscular, and strong, Commodus seemed intent on proving himself in the gladiatorial games, where he fought several bouts a day with other gladiators and wild beasts.

Where Nero had fancied himself a master of all things stage-related, and had acted the part, Commodus took the "emperor-as-eccentric" act one step further and insisted that he was, in fact, the reincarnation of Hercules, the god of strength. In support of this notion, Commodus began to appear in public dressed in the traditional lion-skin mantle of Hercules. This wasn't just megalomania. Commodus was probably trying to convince his subjects that, being a god, further attempts to murder him would be unsuccessful.

Over the last few years of his reign, he denounced and condemned to death scores of senators and their families, claiming that each was guilty of treason for plotting against him.

In the end, Commodus's fear of political murder became, like that of Domitian before him, a self-fulfilling prophecy. Certain that they were in line for execution, several of Commodus's key subordinates joined together with his own mistress, a Christian named Marcia (who feared persecution of both her family and her sect), and had him strangled in his own bath on the eve of one of his interminable gladiatorial contests. The bastard was only thirty-one years old.

⌇

BASTARD'S CALENDAR

Late in his reign, Commodus was so far gone believing his own press that he actually had each of the months in the calendar renamed. After himself. Really. (The months became Amazonius, Invictus, Felix, Pius, Lucius, Aelius, Aurelius, Commodus, Augustus, Herculeus, Romanus, and Exsuperatorius.) As if that weren't enough, when a great fire (yes, another one) devastated Rome in A.D 191 Commodus set himself up as a sort of "second founder" (after the legendary Romulus) and renamed the city "Colonia Commodiana," or "Commodus City."

★54★
DIDIUS JULIANUS
The Man Who Bought the Roman Empire
(A.D. 133–193)

> But what evil have I done? Whom have I killed?
>
> —*Didius Julianus*

Talk about someone born with all of the advantages: well-educated, brought up in the home of an emperor's mother, wanting for nothing, well-married, rich beyond all imagining; successful in politics, a proven military leader—Didius Julianus had it all. Unfortunately, he was clueless. He ought to have known that if you're going to purchase an imperial throne, you can never really count loyalty you paid for.

This is the tragedy of that ultimately foolish bastard, Didius Julianus.

A respected senator during the reign of Commodus, Julianus only escaped execution on a specious charge of treason because that emperor had already killed so many senators as supposed conspirators against his life. After Commodus was murdered and a seasoned army general and politician named Pertinax became emperor, Julianus thrived, rising further in the ranks of the senate, serving in various governmental posts, up to a point where Pertinax at one point publicly proclaimed him "my colleague and successor."

Within months, Pertinax had been murdered by the Praetorian Guard, and his father-in-law Sulpicianus, commander of the Praetorian Guard, was vying for the imperial throne. Julianus won the support of the praetorians (see sidebar) and was proclaimed emperor on March 28, A.D. 193.

The problem for Julianus was that his power base consisted solely of the soldiers he'd bribed, and of not one other person. Within a few short months, several different generals commanding Roman armies out on the frontiers rebelled and had their troops proclaim them emperor, then set about fighting amongst themselves. It was a cycle that would play itself out time and again over the next two hundred years.

The eventual victor in this contest of strong men was Septimius Severus (who has earned his own chapter in this book). Once Severus had consolidated his power and marched on Rome, Julianus, in a panic (and unable to do anything to stop any of the generals who might have actually marched on the capital), offered to share the empire with Severus, naming him co-emperor. Severus responded by having the official carrying Julianus's offer executed.

Julianus swiftly followed, sentenced to death by his beloved senate on June 1, A.D. 193. The Roman author Cassius Dio reports his tearful last words (see the chapter opener); a fitting, if ironic, epitaph for a bastard who ought to have known better.

BASTARD OUTSIDE THE WALL

After Pertinax was murdered, Julianus, encouraged by a number of his senate colleagues, hurried to the praetorian camp to try to win their acclaim as emperor. He was locked out of the camp while their commander, Sulpicianus, was making his own speech asking for their support for his own claim to the vacant imperial throne. Julianus was reduced to shouting his own bids of how much he would pay each praetorian in the auction of their services from outside the wall of their compound.

Once he'd outbid Sulpicianus, Julianus sealed the deal by pointing out to the praetorians that if Sulpicianus succeeded his murdered son-in-law as emperor, he might reasonably be expected to punish the murderers of the previous emperor; the praetorians themselves (never mind Julianus's own ties to his predecessor Pertinax!).

★55★
SEPTIMIUS SEVERUS
The Emperor Who Gave Us the Word "Severe"
(A.D. 145–211)

> There were many things Severus did that were not to our liking, and he was blamed for making the city turbulent through the presence of so many troops and for burdening the State by his excessive expenditures of money, and most of all, for placing his hope of safety in the strength of his army rather than in the good will of his associates in the government.
>
> —*Cassius Dio*, The Roman History

We get any number of words from the Latin, such as the names of most of the months ("July" for Julius Caesar and "August" for Augustus). Imagine what the guy whose name gave us the modern word "severe" must have been like.

Ladies and gentlemen, meet Lucius Septimius Severus, the man who finished the work of earlier ambitious demagogues by turning Rome into the de facto military dictatorship it remained for the last two centuries of its existence.

Severus was that luckiest of men: born in the provinces to an undistinguished family, he rose through the ranks of the empire's civil service because of his family connections. His good luck followed him throughout the next two decades, where he served without merit or particular distinction in a variety of provincial government posts.

In A.D. 191, Severus got particularly lucky: he was appointed governor of Upper Pannonia, which post also carried with it command of the legions defending the Danube frontier against the barbarian tribes to the north.

Two years later, during the tumultuous aftermath of the murder of the emperor Commodus, Severus's troops rose up and proclaimed him emperor. He accepted their proclamation and marched on Rome at the head of his troops, sweeping aside all opposition and entering the city several weeks later.

In order to strengthen his grip on power, the emperor swept aside the largely ornamental senate and expanded the size of the army by hundreds of thousands of men. He used his new legions not just for external but for internal security. He expanded the frontiers in the east and in Britain and crushed the insurrections of two rival generals during the first years of his reign.

It was under Severus that Roman persecution of Christians began in earnest. Where other emperors had executed early church leaders, Severus forbade any resident of the empire from converting to either Judaism or Christianity on pain of death. Thousands were killed and their property confiscated by the state.

Severus died in A.D. 211 after a long illness, leaving a smoothly running military dictatorship to his sons Caracalla and Geta. This bastard's political philosophy can best be summed up by the final advice he gave them: "Agree with each other, give money to the soldiers, and scorn all other men." As we shall see in the next chapter, his sons had a bit of trouble following their ruthless father's advice.

⟂

AFRICAN BASTARD

A Roman citizen from a family that had emigrated a couple of generations earlier, Septimius Severus was born in North Africa, the first Roman emperor not born in Europe. He went to Rome as a young man because two of his cousins were highly placed among the empire's civil servants (both of them serving as consul while Severus was still a child), and these family connections promised him advancement in lucrative government jobs.

★56★
CARACALLA
Don't Drop Your Guard Along with Your Trousers
(A.D. 188–217)

> His mode of life was evil and he was more brutal even than his cruel father. He was gluttonous in his use of food and addicted to wine, hated by his household and detested in every camp save the praetorian guard; and between him and his brother there was no resemblance whatever.
>
> —The Historia Augusta

Calling someone "more brutal even than his cruel father" is saying something when that cruel father was the ruthless Roman emperor Septimius Severus. But in this case it's hardly an exaggeration: the brutal bastard being referred to set up his father-in-law on a charge of treason, eventually executed his wife, and stabbed his own brother to death in the presence of his mother!

While it's true that contemporary and subsequent historians have demonized Caracalla throughout the centuries (his brother Geta was better at spin-doctoring than he was), and he likely wasn't as bad as he's been made out to be, several of the more atrocious misdeeds laid at his feet are probably true.

For starters, Caracalla did set up his father-in-law, who was his father's trusted subordinate, the Praetorian Guard commander Gaius Fulvius Plautianus. He got several centurions to approach old Severus and inform him that Plautianus had attempted to recruit them into a plot to assassinate Severus. Within hours, Plautianus was dead, and his daughter (Caracalla's wife), as the child of a traitor, was sent into exile. Once he was emperor in his own right, Caracalla had her killed.

On his deathbed, Severus had said that Geta and Caracalla ought to share power, and he advised them to trust each other, pay off the army, and not care what anyone else thought. Turns out they were able to accomplish two of those three things.

When it came to trusting each other, though, that was just never going to happen. They loathed each other. Each tried to have the other poisoned within months of their taking the throne in A.D. 211. In their final confrontation, in their mother's chambers, Caracalla stabbed Geta, who died clinging to her.

This was hardly the end of Caracalla's bloody deeds. While he was in Alexandria, he ordered thousands of civilians slaughtered for reasons that remain unclear.

When he invaded the Parthian empire a couple of years later, Caracalla ran out of luck. Some of his personal guardsmen hatched a plot to kill him, which culminated in his being stabbed to death when he stopped by the side of the road to answer the call of nature. When the other members of his retinue turned their backs out of respect for the office, one of their number stepped forward and stabbed Caracalla to death in mid-bowel movement.

BASTARD FASHION STATEMENT

Like Caligula before him, Caracalla derived his nickname from an item of clothing he customarily wore: a caracallus, which was originally a short, tight-fitting cloak with a hood. Caracalla adapted this, making it much longer, and wearing it everywhere he went on campaign with his armies. The soldiers coined his nickname, and as a result he is better known today as Caracalla rather than by his ruling name of Marcus Aurelius Severus Antoninus Pius.

★57★
ELAGABALUS
The Emperor and His Big Stone God
(A.D. 203–222)

> I will not describe the barbaric chants which [Elagabalus],
> together with his mother and grandmother, chanted to [Elaga-
> bal], or the secret sacrifices that he offered to him, slaying boys
> and using charms, in fact actually shutting up alive in the god's
> temple a lion, a monkey and a snake, and throwing in among
> them human genitals, and practicing other unholy rites.
> —*Dio Cassius*, The Roman History

Who was the strangest bastard ever to don the imperial purple of ancient
Rome? How about a gay, cross-dressing religious fanatic who wore more
makeup than most strippers, and allegedly worked as a hooker out of his
rooms in the imperial palace?

Ladies and gentlemen, meet Varius Avitus Bassianus, better known by
the nickname Elagabalus. He ruled the empire under the very Roman-
sounding name of "Marcus Aurelius Antoninus" from A.D. 218 to 222.

Born and raised in Syria, the kid was all of fourteen when his mother and
grandmother used his blood connection to several previous emperors to engi-
neer a claim to the throne. Within months, he was on his way to Rome. And
he literally brought his god with him.

Elagabalus and his followers worshipped a craggy, two-ton phallic-
shaped meteorite as the actual physical incarnation of his god ("Elagabal,"
or "El-Gabal," from which he derived his nickname).

The new emperor's religious views were only part of the problem,
though. Much more important was his penchant for continually thumb-
ing his nose at Rome's traditions—for example, by taking as his husband

a slave-charioteer named Hierocles. He would even go so far as to have his lover catch him "cheating" and beat him: a foreign slave beating a sitting emperor! It couldn't last.

It all finally came to a head in March of A.D. 222, when Elagabalus flew into a rage during a meeting with the commanders of the Praetorian Guard (his personal bodyguard), denouncing them as disloyal: not a very bright thing to do while still standing in the middle of their camp.

They chased him down and killed him in one of the camp latrines. His last words were, "Leave my mother alone!" If those actually were his final wishes, they were ignored. His mother was killed right alongside him. Their bodies were beheaded, dragged through the streets of Rome, and wound up in the Tiber River, the sort of burial that contemporary Roman law reserved for criminals.

Later historians whipped up many improbable tales about this teenaged demagogue, but the truth as we can divine it about Elagabalus is far more interesting.

BASTARD ON PARADE

[Elagabalus] placed the sun god in a chariot adorned with gold and jewels and brought him out from the city to the suburbs. A six-horse chariot carried the divinity, the horses huge and flawlessly white, with expensive gold fittings and rich ornaments. No one held the reins, and no one rode with the chariot; the vehicle was escorted as if the god himself were the charioteer. Elagabalus ran backward in front of the chariot, facing the god and holding the horses' reins. He made the whole journey in this reverse fashion, looking up into the face of his god.

—*Herodian,* History of the Empire from the Death of Marcus Aurelius

★58★
CARINUS
How Screwing Your Employees' Wives Can Cost Ya!
(CA. A.D. 250–285)

> [Carinus] put to death very many innocent men on false charges, seduced the wives of nobles, and even ruined those of his school fellows who had taunted him at school, even with trivial banter.
> —The Historia Augusta

While many Roman emperors had trouble keeping their pants on, Carinus is one of the few whose proclivities actually cost him his life.

That Carinus was a man of ability is beyond doubt. After he became his father's junior co-emperor in A.D. 283, he fought a series of battles first against the Germans on the Rhine frontier, then against the Scots in northern Britain, beating them so soundly that the words "Britannicus Maximus" were added to his imperial title.

When Carinus's father and then his younger brother died under suspicious circumstances while fighting the Parthians on the empire's eastern frontier in A.D. 285, Carinus led his army east to confront Diocletian, the general whom his father's legions had proclaimed emperor in their place.

Along the way, Carinus put down the revolt of a pretender to the throne in northern Italy, again showing considerable strategic ability. The two armies finally met in battle in the Balkans on the River Margus. Carinus had more troops and had the superior strategic position; it seemed as if his winning streak would continue.

That's when several of Carinus's own staff officers took matters into their own hands.

Apparently the emperor had developed a taste for bedding the wives of his subordinates, and wasn't shy about it, having seduced or raped several of them over the previous several months.

Seeing their opportunity and driven by a mixture of anger, fear of what Carinus might do next to them or their families, and a thirst for revenge, these same officers turned on their emperor, cutting him down at his moment of greatest triumph.

With Carinus dead and the fortunate-beyond-all-reason Diocletian inclined to be merciful, the entire army ceased fighting and went over to the other side. Because Diocletian won the day, his propagandists got to tell the story, and Carinus went from being a boss who couldn't keep his hands (and other things) off of the "help" to the cartoonish bastard portrayed in *The Historia Augusta*.

BASTARD PROPAGANDA

That scandal sheet of ancient sources, *The Historia Augusta*, claims of Carinus that "it would be too long to tell more, even if I should desire to do so, about his excesses." This after laying out a smorgasbord of sins on Carinus's part: that he married and divorced no less than nine wives in succession (outdoing fellow bastard Henry VIII of England), some of them while still pregnant with his offspring; that he possessed a voracious bisexual appetite; that basically he screwed everything with a pulse that came within reach; and of course that "he defiled himself by unwonted vices and inordinate depravity," and that "he set aside all the best among his friends and retained or picked out all the vilest." The reality is that he only had one wife of record, and he likely wasn't as bad as painted in this source.

★59★
DIOCLETIAN
The Best Place to Be Standing When Lightning Strikes Your Boss
(A.D. 245–311)

> Diocletian was an author of crimes and a deviser of evil; he ruined everything and could not even keep his hands from God. In his greed and anxiety he turned the world upside down.
>
> —*Lactantius*, De Mortibus Persecutorum ("On the Deaths of the Persecutors")

The son of a former slave, Gaius Aurelius Valerius Diocles was a career soldier who worked his way up through the ranks—first as Roman provincial governor, then as commander of emperor's cavalry bodyguards, and finally as emperor.

Diocletian brought nearly a century of warfare to an end, and reorganized the empire so that it was ruled by two senior emperors (augusti) and two junior emperors (caesars), stabilizing it for the first time in decades. When he retired (another rarity for Roman emperors in any era) in A.D. 305, Diocletian was universally hailed as the restorer of the Roman Empire.

Just how did Diocletian make the leap from chief bodyguard of an emperor to emperor himself? Simple: he made a deal with an equally ambitious army officer willing to help with the planning and the heavy lifting.

This officer was none other than the praetorian prefect (commander of the Praetorian Guard) Arrius Aper, perfectly placed to take out the emperor Carus and his son Numerian. Carus and Numerian were fighting in Parthia (in modern-day Iran). One day just a few months into the campaign, Carus was found dead as a stone in his tent the morning after a fierce thunderstorm. Aper let it out that the emperor had died from being struck by lightning.

137

Really.

Numerian was immediately hailed as emperor and continued the war against Parthia, with inconclusive results. In the spring of A.D. 284, Numerian began to make his way back to Rome. The journey took months. Numerian eventually began to stick to his litter with the blinds pulled, because, as Aper explained to those around him, the young emperor was suffering from an infection of the eyes.

———————————— ⟋⟍ ————————————

PERSECUTING BASTARD

Diocletian and his caesar Galerius carried out an escalating series of persecutions of the Christian sect during his twenty years of rule. Among these acts were the burning of Christian churches, the dismissal of any army officer proven to be a Christian, and the jailing of leading Christians, insisting that they could be released as soon as they sacrificed to Rome's ancient state deities. Those Christians who refused to do this were tortured and killed.

As the army neared the city of Nicomedia in modern-day Turkey, the stench of decaying corpse emanating from the emperor's litter proved too powerful to ignore. Several soldiers opened the litter and found Numerian dead. No one was sure how long he'd been rotting away.

Aper claimed he'd died of natural causes, and immediately called for Numerian's troops to proclaim him his successor. Standing in competition was none other than Diocles. In a meeting held in front of the entire army, a vote was taken during which the soldiers loudly proclaimed the popular Diocles (who equally quickly adopted the more grand sounding name of "Diocletian" as his ruling name) as emperor.

Diocletian's first act was to disavow any complicity in the death of his predecessor. His second was to draw his sword there on the platform where he had just been acclaimed moments before, turn, and kill his rival (and co-conspirator) on the spot, claiming that Aper was the guilty one!

While the depth of Diocletian's involvement in this double plot on the imperial house of Carus is unknown, it's pretty clear that he was involved at some point, and in the end, profited the most from it.

Profiting bastard.

★60★
CONSTANTINE THE GREAT
The Next Best Thing to Being God
(A.D. 272–337)

> With such impiety pervading the human race, and the State threatened with destruction, what relief did God devise? . . . I myself was the instrument he chose. . . . [W]ith God's help I banished and eliminated every form of evil then prevailing, in the hope that the human race, enlightened through me, might be recalled to a proper observance of God's holy laws.
>
> —*Constantine the Great, quoted by Eusebius in* De Vita Constantini

The first Christian emperor of Rome, the man who reunited the empire following the chaotic unraveling of Diocletian's tetrarchy into a decade of civil war, Flavius Julius Constantinus, son of one of the tetrarchs, comes across in the quote above as a ruler with one outsized ego.

No surprise then that he was a paranoid who trusted no one and killed off most of those close to him.

In A.D. 312, Constantine supposedly experienced a revelation leading him to convert to Christianity the night before the Battle of the Milvian Bridge (in northern Rome), a decisive victory over rival imperial claimant Maxentius that left Constantine the most powerful man in the Roman world. After he consolidated his power by first defeating and then killing all of the other claimants to the imperial throne, Constantine set about making Christianity the most powerful religion in the Roman Empire, reversing the policies of previous emperors, who had persecuted Christians. Constantine instead persecuted pagans.

By the mid-320's, Constantine had an heir-apparent ready to step into his shoes; his eldest son Crispus was already an experienced general, popular with the army, and also the focus of growing jealousy and suspicion on the part of his father. It was a tense situation when the imperial entourage headed for Rome in A.D. 326 with the empress Fausta (daughter and sister respectively of Constantine's rivals Maximian and Maxentius, one killed on her husband's order and the other killed fighting him in battle), Crispus, Constantia (Constantine's half-sister and the widow of his rival Licinius), and Licinius's son Licinianus in tow.

At some point during the visit, Constantine's simmering envy and paranoia exploded in a bloodbath. Crispus and Licinianus were arrested on charges of conspiring to depose Constantine and usurp the throne. A few days later, they were executed. A week later, the empress was also put to death on Constantine's order. The evidence against all of these conspirators is scanty. Whether they were guilty of anything is open for debate. But with a ruthless, paranoid nut like Constantine running things, and them likely in constant fear for their own lives, who'd really blame them if they did plot against the emperor?

When Constantine finally died after a long illness in A.D. 337, having reigned for thirty-one years, his court carried on as if he were still alive for three months. Maybe they wanted to be sure that the crazy bastard was actually dead before they worked out the problem of who would succeed him?

ACTUAL BASTARD BASTARD

Constantine was the product of his father Constantius Chlorus's union with a tavern-keeper's daughter named Helena. Whether or not he actually bothered to marry her is open to some conjecture. Regardless, Chlorus swiftly set Helena aside in order to enter into a political marriage with the daughter of one of the other tetrarchs as part of an attempted shoring up of Diocletian's succession plan.

★61★
CONSTANTIUS II
The Emperor as Paranoid Plodder
(A.D. 317–361)

> If any persons should be proved to devote their attention to sacrifices or to worship images, We command that they shall be subjected to capital punishment.
> —*Constantius II*, The Edict of Milan

The Roman emperor Constantius II was hard-working, austere, and methodical, something of a plodder who, according to one ancient historian, "was too dull-witted to make a speaker, and when he turned to versifying produced nothing worthwhile." Yet, when it came to religious toleration or perceived threats to his own life, this otherwise mediocre emperor proved to be every bit the bastard his father, Constantine the Great, had been.

Like his father, Constantius took great interest in religious matters. But where his father had bent Christian doctrine to will and subordinated it to his political purposes, Constantius II found himself buffeted by competing claims of various church fathers.

Constantius was not his father. He wasn't all that bright, and had a short attention span, deferring much of the policymaking during his reign to a number of self-serving imperial eunuchs who enriched themselves at the state's expense. In fact, Constantius himself wasn't even an orthodox Christian. He followed the so-called Arian heresy that emphasized the humanity of Christ.

But that didn't stop him from persecuting non-Christians!

Late in his reign, with no children of his own, Constantius, who had helped wipe out all but one of his cousins while still new to the throne, adopted as his heir the one cousin who hadn't died in his earlier purge: a philosopher named Julian. But when Julian proved very adept at both commanding troops in the field and running a government, Constantius turned on him, disinherited him, and was about to meet him in battle to decide the question when he suddenly took sick and died at the relatively youthful age of forty-three.

—————————— ⟳ ——————————

PARANOID BASTARD

As a young man, the Roman historian Ammianus Marcelinus served as an officer in the army of the emperor Constantius II and knew him personally. The portrait he paints of Constantius's attitudes towards his own position as emperor is telling: "Although in most respects he was comparable to other emperors of average merit, yet if he discovered any ground, however false or slight, for suspecting an attempt upon the throne he showed in endless investigations regardless of right or wrong a cruelty which easily surpassed that of Gaius [Caligula] and Domitian and Commodus. Indeed, at the very beginning of his reign he rivaled their barbarity by destroying root and branch all who were connected with him by blood and birth. The sufferings of the wretched men accused of infringing or violating his prerogative were increased by the bitter and angry suspicions nourished by the emperor in all such cases. Once he got wind of anything of this kind he threw himself into its investigation with unbecoming eagerness, and appointed merciless judges to preside over such trials. In the infliction of punishment he sometimes tried to prolong the agonies of death, if the victim's constitution could stand it."

If you, my Lord, wish to save your skin, you will have no difficulty in doing so. We are rich, there is the sea, there too are our ships. But consider first whether, when you reach safety, you will not regret that you did not choose death in preference. As for me, I stand by the ancient saying: the purple is the noblest death shroud.

—*The Byzantine Empress Theodora to her husband, Justinian I*

The son of illiterate peasants, Justinian was the ultimate country boy come to the big city to make good. His uncle Justin worked his way up through the army to become commander of the emperor's bodyguard and then emperor himself. And when he was made emperor in A.D. 518, he made his very smart nephew his right-hand man.

While he waited for his own term as emperor, Justinian plotted and intrigued, getting rid of potential rivals for the throne. Not a man of either action or physical courage, he preferred to assassinate or buy enemies off rather than fight them.

Still, as emperor he did many great things: revising the Roman law code, instituting a massive building program, and sending out great generals such as the legendary Belisaurius and Narses to reconquer Italy, Spain, North Africa, and southern France for the empire.

All of this cost money, and Justinian passed those expenses on to the citizenry. The reasonably foreseeable result was that the people would get pissed off and riot.

And when it happened, it happened right in Justinian's backyard, at the Hippodrome, Constantinople's open-air coliseum. Determined to flee, Justinian was shamed into action by his iron-willed wife, the empress Theodora.

He ordered his generals to take their troops to the Hippodrome and put down this riot that had attracted tens of thousands and threatened to spill over into open revolt. This they did with grim efficiency. Narses's troops sealed off the coliseum so that no one within could escape. Then Belisaurius's soldiers were ordered inside, where they killed every single living thing within.

The final death toll? Thirty thousand dead in one day.

Justinian's subjects never forgot the example he made of those who rioted during that bloody week. He went on to rule for another thirty-three years. He never taxed his subjects as heavily as he had before the Nike riots (as they were called). And they never again rose up in such open revolt.

THE STEEL IN THE BASTARD'S SPINE

Born into the lowest of circumstances in Constantinople, Theodora was the daughter of a bear-keeper in the Hippodrome who worked by turns as an actress, acrobat, and prostitute before becoming the kept woman of a series of government officials, culminating in her liaison with Justinian, who insisted on marrying her. When he took the imperial throne in A.D. 529, she was very much his partner in ruling. As demonstrated by her speech quoted above, Theodora was a formidable woman, often stiffening her cowardly husband's spine in moments when he wavered. Without her, he might well have fled the city during the Nike riots and lost both his throne and his life. Instead he ensured that thousands of citizens lost theirs in the Hippodrome.

★63★
CHARLEMAGNE
Literal Bastard, Figurative Bastard
(A.D. 742–814)

Charles did not cease, after declaring war, until he had exhausted
King Desiderius by a long siege, and forced him to surrender
at discretion; driven his son Adalgis, the last hope of the Lombards, not only from his kingdom, but from all Italy; restored to
the Romans all that they had lost; subdued Hruodgaus, Duke of
Friuli, who was plotting revolution; reduced all Italy to his power,
and set his son Pepin as king over it.
—*Einhard*, The Life of Charlemagne

There can be little doubt that Charlemagne was a great man. Uniting the
Franks and expanding the Frankish kingdom to its greatest extent, he
helped rekindle the flame of education, even though he himself could
barely read. A great warrior, he stood off the Muslims in Spain and converted heathens in central Europe to Christianity.

Like all great men, Charlemagne had a bit of the bastard in him.

The passage quoted above shows some of that bastardry and determination.
Charlemagne went into northern Italy and conquered the Lombards because
their king was harboring a party of Frankish nobles that included a rival for
the Frankish throne. This rival was named Pippin, and he was the eldest son of
Charlemagne's dead brother, Carloman.

Because of Frankish succession traditions, Charlemagne didn't inherit
King Pepin the Short's kingdom outright upon his father's death in A.D. 768.
Instead, he split it with his younger brother Carloman.

The two brothers despised each other. They began preparing for war over the kingdom, which was only narrowly avoided by Carloman's sudden death as a result of a nosebleed.

When a deputation of Carloman's own nobles appealed to Charlemagne to annex Carloman's territory rather than allow his underage son to succeed him, Charlemagne did so, effectively cutting Carloman's sons out of the succession. Carloman's widow Gerberga responded by taking her two sons and fleeing to Lombardy (in northern Italy), seeking protection from Desiderius, the king of the Lombards. In A.D. 773, Charlemagne, no doubt realizing what a potential threat they represented to his hold on the Frankish throne, went after them.

What resulted from all of this was the end of the Lombard kingdom in Italy (Charlemagne gave it to the pope after he finished conquering it). The king of the Lombards and his entire family were forced to become monks or nuns (at least they weren't put to death). And Gerberga and her sons? No further mention is made of them in the Frankish chronicles. Modern scholars assume they too were forced to take the tonsure and the veil.

――――――――――――― ∽ ―――――――――――――

BASTARD SUCCESSION

The early Frankish kings did not hand over their realms in one piece to their eldest sons. Instead, according to custom, they split their kingdoms among their living sons. Charlemagne himself only had one son survive to adulthood, but that son, Louis, split the Frankish kingdom among his own three sons, leading to the foundation of the separate kingdoms of France and Germany.

★64★
EMPRESS IRENE OF BYZANTIUM
Sometimes a Boy's Best Friend Is His Mother. This Isn't One of Those Times
(CA. A.D. 752–803)

> Scheming and duplicitous, consumed by a devouring ambition and an insatiable lust for power, [Irene] was to bring dissension and disaster to the Empire for nearly a quarter of a century, and to leave a still darker stain on her reputation by one of the foulest murders that even Byzantine history has to record.
>
> —*Modern historian John Julius Norwich in* Byzantium: The Apogee

By all accounts beautiful, strong-willed, narrow-minded, ambitious, and ruthless, the Byzantine Empress Irene was so obsessed with power that she kept her hands on the reins long after they should by right have passed to her son. When he asserted himself and insisted on getting his birthright, she had him ambushed, seized, kidnapped, and blinded in order to retain her throne.

Married young to the weak-willed and tubercular emperor Leo IV, Irene survived him by many years, taking over as regent for their ten-year-old son Constantine when he succeeded his father in A.D. 780. For the next decade, Irene ran the empire right into a ditch.

It wasn't entirely her fault. The empire at the time was riven by a religious controversy centuries in the making over the question of whether or not the sacred icons used in worship services were in fact idols that turned all prayer into a blasphemy. Irene, an orthodox ruler, favored the use of icons. The problem was that the majority of her best soldiers and most able military commanders were iconoclasts ("idol smashers") and disagreed. This, added to her profligate spending, led to a whole lot of conflict.

Included among the iconoclasts was Irene's own son, the emperor Constantine VI. Growing up to be nearly as much of a weak-willed nonentity as his father, Constantine did at one point briefly muster up enough gumption to stand up to Mommy, depose her, and send her off to exile. It didn't last long. Within a year, she returned to the capital city of Constantinople and to her previous position as co-emperor with her son.

Things came to a head the second time it looked to Irene as if her son was about to stand up for himself. She had her son kidnapped, and on Tuesday, August 15, A.D. 797, she ordered his eyes put out. It was done in the purple-lined birthing room where he had been born! He soon died from the brutality.

Remarkably, Irene managed to hold on to power for six years after her son's death (she claimed he was actually alive and in prison for treason). Eventually, she was deposed in a palace coup and sent into exile on the island of Lesbos. She died of natural causes a year later.

⌇

WHAT'S IN A BASTARD'S NAME?

The Greek name Irene comes from the word *eirine*, which means "peace." The irony of this violent and ruthless woman's choice of regnal name (her given name is lost to us) is palpable. Perhaps it was to be expected, though, from a tough customer of a queen mother who insisted on using the title of basileus ("emperor") rather than basilissa ("empress").

★65★
POPE STEPHEN VI
Even Death Can't Stop Justice
(A.D. ?–897)

Read, — how there was a ghastly Trial once/Of a dead man by a
live man, and both, Popes
—*Robert Browning*, The Ring and the Book

No less than twenty-five men served as pope between the years A.D. 872
and 972. During this time, Rome's wealthy families vied with each other
to see one of their number don the shoes of the fisherman and in turn dis-
pense ridiculous amounts of patronage among his kinsmen.

Feuds developed; blood was spilled. In the midst of all of this chaos,
enter Pope Stephen VI, who went beyond the pale.

He ordered a predecessor's corpse dug up and put on trial.

A succession of popes—including Stephen VI—made outside alliances
with powerful Italian families for military support. They cemented these
alliances by legitimizing the rule of the ally in question through a for-
mal papal coronation. One pope who had done this was a predecessor of
Stephen's named Formosus, whose reign lasted five years (A.D. 891–896).
During that time, Formosus (whose name in Latin means, "good looking")
had crowned the young duke of Spoleto as Holy Roman Emperor, then
turned around and offered the same crown to Arnulf, king of Germany.

Arnulf had answered Formosus's invitation by invading Italy and taking Rome. Formosus promptly crowned him Holy Roman Emperor as well.
Needless to say, this caused an uproar in Spoleto. Formosus responded by
dying shortly afterward. He was succeeded by a couple of popes with ridicu-
lously short reigns (one of them only lasted two weeks), and eventually by

Stephen VI, in hock up to his eyeballs to his political patrons: Spoleto's ruling family.

About six months into his reign, Stephen had Formosus dug up and propped up in a chair in the Vatican. Formosus was then placed on trial with Pope Stephen himself sitting as judge. Formosus (or rather his corpse) was accused of (among other things) being ambitious enough to actually want to be pope (the nerve!). No one is sure of Stephen's reasons for putting on this, the ultimate show trial, but he did suffer from some well-documented psychosis and was almost certainly feeling pressure from his Spoleto sponsors.

THE CADAVER SYNOD

Called the "Synod Horrenda" in Church Latin, this "Cadaver Synod" resulted in riots throughout Rome, which eventually cost Stephen first his papal throne and eventually his life. He was strangled in prison less than six months after condemning the dead Formosus.

The trial lasted for weeks, during which time Stephen would frequently interrupt his own papal prosecutor in order to rant at Formosus's moldering corpse, calling it all manner of names, accusing it of murder, blasphemy, and several other crimes with which it was not actually charged. How the corpse responded is not recorded.

The trial's outcome was a foregone conclusion. The corpse was stripped of its expensive papal vestments, the first three fingers of its right hand (the three with which a pope blesses his subjects) were cut off, and the body was briefly reburied, this time in an unmarked grave in a cemetery reserved for foreigners. Within a couple of days it had been dug up yet again and tossed in the Tiber River, only to be pulled out by a monk loyal to the dead pope's memory.

Once again, Formosus's reaction, if any, to this news is not recorded.

★66★
BASIL I
"THE MACEDONIAN"
OF BYZANTIUM
Why Trusting Your Life to an Assassin Probably Isn't a Good Idea
(CA. A.D. 830–886)

> I have got rid of the fox; but in his place I have put a lion who will end by devouring us all.
> —*Bardas, caesar of the Byzantine Empire*

Bardas, quoted above, as regent to Michael III, was the Byzantine emperor in everything but name and had gotten rid of one threat to his power. An unintended consequence was Basil's elevation as Michael's successor. Within a couple of years, Bardas's pronouncement would prove eerily prophetic, because Basil, completely illiterate (when a signature was required, he signed by tracing it through a stencil, just Charlemagne), but strong as an ox and cunning as a sphinx, went on to assassinate Bardas, take his place, then turn on his mentor Michael, murder him as well, take his throne, establish the so-called Macedonian Dynasty of Byzantine emperors, and rule for nineteen years as Basil I.

As high chamberlain, Basil was expected to sleep in the emperor's bedroom (usually this was a post filled only by eunuchs, incapable of sex), which set tongues wagging about whether or not the two men, seemingly inseparable, might be having a sexual relationship (unlikely, but this is gossip we're talking about). Regardless, he was able to poison Michael's tiny mind against his uncle Bardas, convincing him that the older man was out to assassinate him and take the throne for himself.

So Michael agreed to allow Basil to handle the situation. While the three of them were on a military campaign to retake the island of Crete from the Arabs, Basil made his move. As the three sat down to listen to morning reports, Basil suddenly gave Bardas a sucker punch that knocked him to the ground. Within a minute, he was dead as Basil's guards hurried in with swords to finish him off.

When the army returned to Constantinople, Michael proclaimed Basil as his co-emperor.

And how did Basil repay this show of faith?

About a year after he became co-emperor, Basil and a group of his fellow palace officials snuck into the emperor's bedchamber and stabbed him to death (first cutting his hands off). The people didn't seem to mind; Basil had demonstrated himself a capable (if illiterate) leader, and Michael, a hopeless incompetent and blackout drunk, was not the type of emperor over the loss of whom most taxpayers would lose much sleep.

Basil ruled wisely and well once he actually became emperor, presiding over a period of peace and prosperity unparalleled in the long history of the Byzantine Empire. Considered one of the greatest of the empire's rulers, he definitely showed his bastard side in clearing the way for his own ascent to ultimate power!

∽

BASTARD GEOGRAPHY LESSON

In spite of the nickname, Basil wasn't Macedonian. He was Armenian. Like many subjects of the empire, his parents had been forcibly resettled from their native Armenia to a part of Thrace where mostly Macedonians lived. Once he got to Constantinople and in good with the emperor, the nickname stuck. In fact, the royal dynasty he founded bears the name "The Macedonian Dynasty" as a result.

★67★
BASIL II OF BYZANTIUM
What It Takes to Earn the Title
of "Bulgar Slayer"
(A.D. 958–1025)

> Basil was ugly, dirty, coarse, boorish, totally philistine and almost
> pathologically mean. He was, in short, profoundly un-Byzantine.
> . . . He cared only for the greatness and prosperity of his Empire.
> No wonder that in his hands it reached its apogee."
> —*John Julius Norwich*, Byzantium: The Apogee

The Byzantine Empire, that Greek-speaking successor state of Rome that
flourished in the eastern Mediterranean for hundreds of years after the end
of Roman power in the west, saw more than its share of imperial bastards,
rulers capable of great works and great cruelty, frequently all at the same
time. Without question the most remarkable of these was a great military
leader who sold his sister to a foreign ruler in exchange for military support, and blinded fifteen thousand captive enemy soldiers all at once, in
order to break the resistance of a previously implacable foe.

Ladies and gentlemen, meet Basil II, who ruled the empire from the
time he was two until his death sixty-five years later.

During his reign, Basil shared his throne with two regents (each of whom
married his mother, the dowager empress Theophano) and with his younger
brother Constantine VIII. After the death of his final regent, the general John
Tzimiskes in A.D. 976, the eighteen-year-old Basil was finished sharing power
(his ineffectual younger brother would prove nothing more than a figurehead).
For the next forty-nine years, there was no question who called the shots in the
empire: Basil.

The learning curve as emperor was steep, and Basil made many costly mistakes early on, including a humiliating defeat by Bulgarian troops that necessitated signing away vast amounts of territory along the Danube River and the payment of a ridiculous amount of tribute. But like all intelligent leaders, the young emperor learned from his mistakes, and he was so disciplined, so single-minded, that he would allow nothing to stand in the way of his bringing the empire's enemies (both internal and external) to heel.

Fighting a long costly civil war with a number of his nobles in what is now Turkey, Basil eventually defeated them with the help of Vladimir I, the grand prince of Kiev. Vladimir's price for his military support was steep: he wanted the emperor's own sister Anna as his bride. Basil eventually sent her off to a tearful wedding to the "northern barbarian," a ruthless move that saved his empire.

Free at last to deal with the Bulgarians and their tsar, Samuel, who had so humiliated him years before, Basil finally defeated them in a pitched battle at Kleidon, where his army took 15,000 Bulgar captives. Basil's revenge was devastating: He blinded the captives and sent them back to their tsar.

To this day the Greeks refer to their greatest emperor as "Basil Bulgaroktonos": "Basil the Bulgar Slayer." Guess "Bulgar Blinder" doesn't have quite the same ring to it.

ACTUAL BASTARD?

Basil II might have literally been one of history's great bastards. Put simply, Basil didn't look or act much like either of his parents. Where his mother was dark-haired and dark-eyed and his scholarly, intellectual father was tall, thin, and had a long black beard, Basil was of medium height, barrel-chested, blonde, and blue-eyed. There has been much speculation that Basil was actually the product of an adulterous union between his mother and one of the imperial palace's mercenary Viking guardsmen (known as Varangians).

EADWIG OF ENGLAND
Screwing His Kingdom Away
(A.D. 941?–959)

Shameful to relate, people say that in his turn [Eadwig] acted wantonly with [Aethelgifu and her daughter Aelfgifu], with disgraceful caresses, without any decency on the part of either. And when at the time appointed by all the leading men of the English he was anointed and consecrated king by popular election, on that day after the kingly anointing at the holy ceremony, the lustful man suddenly jumped up and left the happy banquet and the fitting company of his nobles, for the aforesaid caresses of loose women.
—The Life of St. Dunstan

In A.D. 955, a teenaged pretty-boy inherited the English crown. History is filled with the stories of underaged kings hustled to the throne after the untimely death of their predecessors. What makes the case of young Eadwig remarkable is that on the very day he took the throne he got caught in the middle of a threesome with a cousin and her mother while his coronation feast was still going on in another wing of the castle!

A direct descendant of Alfred the Great, Eadwig was so physically handsome that the common people referred to him as "All-Fair." A child when his father Edmund I died and still in his teens when he succeeded his uncle Eadred as sovereign, Eadwig was either a foolish, horny teenager or an independent-minded rebel trying to curb the might of a very powerful clergy, or some combination of the two.

Either way, tongues started wagging when Dunstan, the prominent abbot who supposedly caught the king *in flagrante*, was summarily banished, followed closely by a royal wedding between the king and the younger of his two partners.

If Eadwig hoped to silence public opinion by marrying Aelfgifu and exiling Dunstan, he was doomed to disappointment. Within two years, his marriage had been annulled on the grounds that he and his wife were too closely related. The portion of his kingdom north of the Thames River had successfully rebelled, seceded from the kingdom, and selected Eadwig's younger brother Edgar as its king.

Two years later in A.D. 959, Eadwig died under mysterious circumstances. He was not yet twenty years old.

—————————— ✆ ——————————

THE BASTARD VERSUS THE SAINT

In the case of King Eadwig, everything we know about his conflict with the abbot Dunstan comes down to us from clerical chroniclers. Think it's possible they had an axe to grind?

So did Eadwig actually do the deed? Abbot Dunstan and another churchman supposedly discovered the king with his pants down when they were sent by the other nobles at the ceremony to bring him back to the feast he had so hastily departed.

According to "B," the all-but-anonymous priest who wrote about the incident in florid detail, the two clergymen "found the royal crown, which was bound with wondrous metal, gold and silver and gems, and shone with many-coloured luster, carelessly thrown down on the floor, far from [King Eadwig's] head, and he himself repeatedly wallowing between the two [women] in an evil fashion, as if in a vile sty." Outraged, the two men insisted the king return with them to the ceremony, eventually dragging Eadwig "from the women by force."

★69★
POPE BENEDICT IX
The Man Who Sold the Papacy
(CA. A.D. 1012–CA.1056)

That wretch, from the beginning of his pontificate to the end of
his life, feasted on immorality.
—*St. Peter Damian*, Liber Gomorrhianus

Who in their right mind gives the sort of wealth and power that goes with
being pope to a twenty-year-old and doesn't expect it to go straight to the
kid's head? Who doesn't expect someone living the medieval equivalent of a
rock-star life to go a bit nuts?

A bunch of well-bribed Catholic church leaders, that's who. Because
in the case of medieval Pope Benedict IX, this is precisely what happened.

The younger son of a powerful Italian nobleman, Benedict was elected pope in
A.D. 1032 after his father bribed the papal electors in order to ensure it.

Daddy's purchase of the papacy had a profound effect on young Benedict.
Cynical and capricious from the start, Benedict's rule was quickly marked by
episodes that illustrated not only his complete disregard for either tradition
or propriety but his taste for wretched excess as well.

He earned scorn by selling church offices for hefty bribes (an offense
known as "simony"), hosting frequent bisexual orgies, and even going so far
as to curse God and toast the Devil at every meal!

For his part, Benedict doesn't seem to have given a damn what his critics
thought. His power base was among the members of the Roman aristocracy,
and as long as they backed him, he felt free to do as he pleased. Turned out
he reckoned without the powerful (and fickle) Roman mob, who rioted in
A.D. 1036 and ran Il Papa right out of the Eternal City. The uprising was

quickly put down and Benedict returned to power, but he never completely regained control of the city.

By the time Benedict's opponents within the church had succeeded in driving him from Rome a second time in A.D. 1045, Benedict had tired of being pope. So he offered to sell the papacy to his godfather and chief advisor, a well-respected priest named Johannes Gratianus ("John Gratian") for a ridiculous sum meant to fund a proposed lifestyle change.

***

MURDERING BASTARD

Most of Benedict's opponents considered their reigning head of the church something of a bogeyman, perpetrator of "many vile adulteries and murders." Desiderius of Monte Cassino, a contemporary of Benedict IX who later reigned as Pope Victor III, wrote that Benedict committed "rapes, murders, and other unspeakable acts." Benedict's reign, wrote Desiderius, was "so vile, so foul, so execrable that I shudder to think of it."

The older man accepted and took the papal name of Gregory VI. The bribe he gave Benedict so completely bankrupted the papal treasury that for months afterward the church was unable to pay its bills. To further complicate matters, Benedict's foes among the clergy refused to recognize Gregory's right to the succession, electing one of their number pope as Sylvester III.

So technically Benedict left not one but two popes (well, really a pope and a pretender, or antipope) behind in Rome. Within weeks, he'd run through his new fortune and promptly headed back to Rome, trying to get his old job back. This time his allies deserted him, and Benedict got booted from the city yet again.

By A.D. 1047, Henry III (the Holy Roman Emperor) had seen enough. With the support of a majority of the church's bishops, the emperor convened a special church council that settled the question by giving all three men the boot. A year later, Benedict was charged with simony (a charge of which he was clearly guilty). When he refused to appear before the church court that indicted him, Benedict was excommunicated.

At some point during the next decade, the ex-pope had a change of heart and presented himself at the abbey of Santa Maria di Grottaferrata, begging for God's forgiveness. He spent the remainder of his days as a monk in that abbey, dying there in A.D. 1065.

Repentant bastard.

★70★
WILLIAM I THE CONQUEROR
Sounds Better Than "William the Bastard"
(CA. A.D. 1028–1087)

He was over all measure severe to the men who gainsaid his
will. He was a very rigid and cruel man, so that no man durst do
anything against his will. . . . He had earls in his bonds who had
acted against his will; bishops he cast from their bishoprics, and
abbots from their abbeys; and thanes he kept in prison; and at
last he spared not his own brother.

—The Anglo-Saxon Chronicle

The man who conquered England in order to press a weak claim to its
throne was born a literal bastard in Normandy (northern France) around
A.D. 1028 to Robert I, Duke of Normandy, and a woman named Herleva.
Before his death in A.D. 1087, he proved one of the most ruthless bastards
of the Middle Ages, taking an independent kingdom and turning it into a
personal fiefdom. In more high-fallutin' language: a conqueror.

William hosted his cousin Edward the Confessor (later king of England)
while the latter was in exile, and claimed after the Confessor's death that
he had promised to make William his heir. When Harold Godwinson was
selected to be king instead, William invaded England, famously defeating
the English at the Battle of Hastings in A.D. 1066. With Harold killed in
the battle (arrow in the eye), there was no one to stand in William's way,
and he was crowned king on Christmas Eve of that year.

What followed were six years of consolidating power through replacing high-level Anglo-Saxon church and government leaders with his own family members and drinking buddies, and putting down rebellion after rebellion through a series of bloody campaigns and fierce reprisals. A telling indicator of William's success in grabbing the levers of power in England and holding on with both hands: when he was crowned king, the landowning aristocracy in the kingdom (called thegns) numbered around 4,000, all of them Anglo-Saxons. By the year he died, that number had been reduced to two.

William doesn't seem to have been all that interested in actually living in England once he'd conquered it. Instead, he used the kingdom both to reward followers with grants of land and titles and as a giant piggy bank to fund his far-more-important-to-him wars against the king of France, his neighbors in Flanders and Anjou, and (of course) his own rebellious son, Robert Curthose, who went on to succeed him as duke of Normandy on his death.

Grown morbidly obese in his later years, William sustained life-threatening injuries in a fall from a horse while (go figure) campaigning in France in A.D. 1087. Lingering near death for several weeks, he had time to both regret and confess his sins, reportedly saying at one point: "I am stained with the rivers of blood that I have spilled."

He died shortly afterward, and during his funeral service his already corpulent decomposing body swelled to such a size that it broke open his coffin and sickened the assembled mourners with the stench it gave off. An ironic footnote to the life of the grandson of an undertaker!

***

YET ANOTHER LITERAL BASTARD

Referred to by even his own subjects in France as "Guillaume-le-Batard" ("William the Bastard"), the future King William I of England was constantly reminded (especially by his foes) that the family business of his maternal grandfather was that of an embalmer.

★71★
ODO OF BAYEUX
When Your Vows Forbid You to Shed Blood, Use a Big, Heavy Club Instead
(CA. A.D. 1030–1097)

> God forbid that I should touch the Bishop of Bayeux,
> but I make the Earl of Kent my prisoner.
> —*William I the Conqueror of England*

The younger half-brother of William the Conqueror, Odo went from being the bishop of a minor holding in Normandy to the second-most-powerful man in England in less than a year. Once ensconced as William's regent (and earl of Kent), Odo ran the country with little interference from his brother, as long as he kept sending the new king plenty of revenue from his conquered subjects. Odo took the opportunity to skim from the tax revenues, making himself wealthy and powerful enough to fancy himself a viable candidate for pope.

Though a priest is forbidden to shed blood, Odo was an active participant in both the planning and the execution of his brother William's invasion of England in A.D. 1066. In battle, he wore armor and carried a heavy oaken club that he used as a weapon in place of a sword (thereby getting around the whole "shedding blood" thing).

In recognition of Odo's crucial assistance, William made him his regent. It was Odo who set about consolidating his brother's conquest, centralizing the government, and serving, in addition to all of his other duties, as England's first chief justice.

By the early 1180s, Odo had amassed such wealth and made so many connections that he dared to dream that he might one day go where neither Frenchman nor Englishman (since as a Norman he was technically both) had gone before: getting elected pope. At about this time, he began laying the groundwork for taking the Holy See: buying a villa in Rome, laying out massive amounts of gold in the form of bribes to the large number of church officials whose support would be needed if he were to become pontiff, even hiring a small mercenary army to protect himself and his interests once he became pope.

Once William got wind of Odo's pontifical ambitions, he came back to England himself, took one look at the books (because no earl, no matter how powerful, ought to have been able to afford the outlays that Odo had been making!), and called kid brother to account.

Odo languished in prison for years until William's death in A.D. 1187. Freed by William's son William II Rufus, Odo promptly set about rebelling against the new king, supporting the claims of his older (and more pliable) brother Robert. The rebellion was crushed and Odo was banished. Eventually going on crusade, he died in Sicily on his way to the Holy Land in A.D. 1097.

───────── ✑ ─────────

BASTARD JUSTICE

Since the office of chief justice was newly created by the Conqueror, no one was sure just how far the duties of the person filling the position should extend. In Odo's case, he wasn't just the highest-ranking legal officer in the realm, he also served as both the head tax man and the de facto finance minister. In an interesting bit of unsurprising irony, one of only two surviving records of a court case involving Odo by name is a case in which he appeared not as presiding judge but as the defendant in trial involving the illegal seizure of church land. He was found guilty and had to forfeit the land and make restitution.

★72★
HENRY IV OF GERMANY
How Much Penance Can One King Do?
(A.D. 1050–1106)

I want there to be no peasant in my kingdom so poor that he cannot have a chicken in his pot every Sunday.
—*Holy Roman Emperor, Henry IV*

The original author of a quote attributed to twentieth-century American bastard populist politician Huey Long was a king who spent his life
and his reign locked in a political struggle with the Catholic Church over
control of both the church itself and most of central Europe. Henry IV
became ruler of the Holy Roman Empire (which was neither "Holy" nor
"Roman" nor truly an "Empire," more a hodgepodge of secular German
and Italian principalities loosely strung together) in his mid-thirties, many
years after he had inherited the German throne (to which he ascended at
the age of six).

Kidnapped at age twelve and forced to serve as the figurehead of a government
run in everything but name by German Catholic Church officials, Henry even
married an heiress chosen by his church masters. Once he reached his majority
(in A.D. 1068), he attempted to divorce her, but threat of excommunication
from the church sufficiently cowed him, and he backed down.

Because Henry had little support from among Germany's nobles, he supported the papacy in its wars against Norman brigands in southern Italy
for much of the next two decades, as he needed the Church's authority to
survive in power.

After becoming Holy Roman Emperor in A.D. 1084, Henry got into
a tug-of-war with the pope, a fellow German named Gregory VII. Henry
wanted to be allowed to appoint high-level churchmen (cardinals, bishops)

to empty positions within Germany himself, instead of accepting the pope's appointments. This was pure politics: clergy who owed their cushy positions to the king were more likely to support the king in disputes with the papacy, whereas papal-appointed clergy would obviously look to Rome for guidance.

Gregory VII responded to Henry's attempt to circumvent papal power by excommunicating him, literally kicking him out of the church. An excommunicated monarch, the pope claimed, was illegitimate in the eyes of God, and his subjects were not required to either pay taxes or obey his laws.

Henry famously did penance by standing outside a mountain castle where the pope was riding out a snowstorm for two days before being granted an audience with the pope. Gregory accepted Henry's penance and reversed his excommunication.

But in A.D. 1105, Henry ran afoul of a different pope (Victor III), who promptly excommunicated him again (this time for going back on the oath he had given Gregory). His own son betrayed him, forcing him to abdicate in his favor. Henry IV died the next year, still attempting to regain his throne.

--- ∽ ---

BASTARD'S SON AND SUCCESSOR

Ironically enough, the son who forcibly deposed Henry IV was his second son, also named Henry, who owed his own position as king of Germany to his father's decision to elevate him to the throne in A.D. 1099 instead of his elder brother Conrad, who was in rebellion against Henry IV at the time. Six years later this "more loyal"(but certainly equally ambitious) of the two sons would betray his own father on the grounds that an excommunicated king had no legitimacy to rule his subjects!

WILLIAM II OF ENGLAND
Red-Headed Bachelor Bastard
(CA. A.D. 1056–1100)

> Through the counsels of evil men, who were always grateful to
> him, and through his own greed, he was always tormenting this
> nation with an army and with unjust taxes. . . . He was hateful to
> almost all his people, and odious to God, as his end made clear.
> —The Anglo-Saxon Chronicle

Nicknamed "Rufus" (Latin for "red") either because of his red hair or
ruddy complexion, William was the third son and chosen successor (as
king of England) of William the Conqueror. A confirmed bachelor in an
age where royal families married their kids off early and often, a religious
skeptic in an age of faith, and quite possibly a gay man in that most clos-
eted of times, the Middle Ages, William Rufus was also a rapacious and
innovative taxer of his subjects, especially the clergy.

Indifferent to the church throughout much of his reign, William Rufus seems
to have looked on it largely as many in his family did—as a source of revenue. When a bishop, abbot, or other high church official died, the king was
supposed to select a successor. But because the monarch was also expected to
maintain and care for the properties of the office in question while seeking out
a worthy successor, he was also allowed to collect the rents, taxes, and other
revenues due the abbey/monastery/other sort of church property in question
in the interim.

William Rufus exploited this loophole as a source of enormous revenue
by simply not bothering to fill vacant church offices within his kingdom.

Like his father before him, William needed a lot of money because he
was constantly fighting in France, and war was expensive. He dreamed of

reuniting his father's realms of England and Normandy by deposing his brother Robert. He got his wish in A.D. 1096, when Robert pawned his duchy to William in return for a large amount of cash to fund his going on the First Crusade.

Whether because of the way he squeezed them for revenues or because of his debauched lifestyle, the contemporary church chroniclers weren't very kind to William Rufus, alleging darkly that the king's court was rampant with all-night drinking parties, frequented by loose women (and men), a haven of lawless, godless knights committed only to a king who promised them easy living, lots of hunting, and enough fighting to enrich themselves at the expense of conquered foes. In other words, pretty much like most other royal courts at the time!

In A.D. 1100, Rufus was out hunting with a bunch of his knights, including his youngest brother, Henry (who'd gotten nothing but money from daddy). In what was later termed a hunting accident, one of his companions killed him with an arrow shot to the chest.

Seizing the initiative, Henry made his way to Winchester, took possession of the royal treasury, had himself crowned king, and buried William at the abbey there.

Right place, right time, huh?

CAPABLE BASTARD

William the Conqueror had quarreled with his incompetent older son Robert for years before he died. Thus it was little surprise to anyone when he left his third son William the throne of England, and forced Robert to settle for the Duchy of Normandy. The Conqueror's last surviving son Henry didn't get any land, just a large cash settlement with which he was directed in the dead king's will to go out and buy some property!

★74★
ENRICO DANDOLO
OF VENICE
The Man Who Hijacked the Fourth Crusade
(A.D. 1107?–1205)

We cannot be sure of his age when, on 1 January 1193, he was raised to the ducal throne.... But even if he was in only his middle seventies, he would still have been, at the time of the Fourth Crusade, an octogenarian of several years' standing. A dedicated, almost fanatical patriot, he had spent much of his life in the service of Venice.

—*John Julius Norwich*, Byzantium: The Apogee

In A.D. 1202, tens of thousands of French and German crusaders camped outside the powerful maritime city-state of Venice. Out of money and with no means to proceed further on their own, they turned to the Venetians and their leader (or "doge") for help.

The doge was a formidable character named Enrico Dandolo. A diplomat of many years' service to the Serene Republic (as the Venetians called it), Dandolo was of advanced age, blind as justice, and cunning beyond expression.

By the time he had died of old age three years later, the octogenarian had manipulated the crusaders into serving as mercenaries for the Venetians in return for passage to their destination, and rerouting their crusade away from the Holy Land to the Christian city of Constantinople.

He even succeeded in gulling the crusade's leaders into thinking it was their own idea!

Why did Dandolo, in this age of faith, wish to attack co-religionists in Constantinople? The answer is simple and illustrative. In Dandolo's view, it seems, the interests of commerce and power politics trumped those of faith. Turns out the Venetians had just signed a lucrative trading treaty with the rulers of Egypt, and had no interest in destabilizing the current regime there. With Constantinople in crusader hands, the Venetians, with their large and powerful fleet, would be unrivaled for control (both political and commercial) of the entire eastern Mediterranean.

Dandolo's scheme turned out better than even he could have foreseen. In A.D. 1204, the knights of the Fourth Crusade did something no one had been able to do in the nine hundred years of Constantinople's existence: they breached the city's huge walls and captured it.

You can guess what happened next: thousands killed, looting on a massive scale, the crusaders squabbling among themselves over their captured booty. And Venice ascendant in the eastern Mediterranean for centuries to come.

And Dandolo? He never returned to Venice. When he died in the city he had helped conquer in A.D. 1205, his countrymen buried him in a corner of the church of Hagia Sophia—a final honor for him, and a final insult to the residents of the city of Constantine.

───────────── ∽ ─────────────

MANIPULATIVE BASTARD

Blind as he was, Dandolo still knew how to put on a show and make the most of an impressive stage. Having convinced the leaders of the Fourth Crusade that it was the decision of the Venetian citizens as to whether to help them, he packed the gorgeous and imposing church of St. Mark with thousands of Venetian citizens for Sunday Mass. As historian Steven Runciman later reported it: "Then the Doge and people raised their hands and cried aloud with a single voice, 'We grant it! We grant it!' And so great was the noise and tumult that the very earth seemed to tremble underfoot."

★75★
HENRY II OF ENGLAND
Putting the "Devil" Into "Devil's Brood"
(A.D. 1133–1189)

> May God let me live until I can have my revenge on you.
> —Henry II's last words to his son and successor Richard I

Imagine a medieval French noble actually wealthier and more powerful than his feudal overlord, the king of France. Now imagine that this noble, already owning more than half of France as his birthright, also won the crown of England, then in turn stole the French king's queen.

Further imagine that this monarch fathered a nest of vipers so disloyal to him, and so contentious with one another, that they were eventually dubbed "the Devil's Brood." Lastly, picture a man so committed to marital gamesmanship that he took a much younger French princess intended as a bride for one of his sons as his own mistress.

Imagine no further. This guy actually lived.

Ladies and gentlemen, meet Henry II: king of England; duke of Aquitaine, Gascony, and Normandy; count of Anjou, Maine, and Nantes; lord of Ireland; husband of the celebrated Eleanor of Aquitaine; and father of both Richard the Lion-Hearted and John I of England.

In A.D. 1173, all four of Henry's sons, egged on by his wife Eleanor of Aquitaine, rebelled against him, allying themselves with the French king Louis VII, who sought the return of his daughter (now Henry's mistress), Princess Alys of France, engaged but never married to Henry's son Richard.

Henry masterfully played his sons off against each other, forcing the most capable of them, then-sixteen-year-old Richard, to do obeisance in order to keep his power base in southern France. Outwitted and outmaneuvered (not for the first or the last time) by his vassal, Louis gave up the fight and sued for peace. For her deeds, Henry kept Eleanor prisoner for the next sixteen years until his own death in A.D. 1189.

Predeceased by two of his sons (Henry the Young King and Duke Geoffrey II of Brittany), betrayed in the end by the one he most favored (John, who has his own chapter in this book), toward the end of his reign, Henry also faced the bitter reality of being beaten at his own conniving game by Louis VII's wily son Philip Augustus. At last outmanned and outmaneuvered, Henry swallowed his pride and acknowledged his third son, Eleanor's favorite, Richard, as his heir and successor. It was at this meeting that the old king quietly spoke the words quoted above even as he made a show of making peace with his son. Even then he was suffering from the fever (likely dysentery) that killed him two days later.

Henry II, royal bastard to the bitter end.

———————————— ☙ ————————————

ATTENTION DEFICIT BASTARD

If Henry Plantagenet lived today, his doctors would likely have prescribed him Ritalin for Attention Deficit Disorder. As king he was famously restless, and would pack up and move the court at a whim, wandering ceaselessly among his many holdings both on the Continent and in England. This applied in diplomatic and military matters as well. With vast holdings in England and France, Henry had difficulty leaving well enough alone, and literally couldn't keep himself from stirring the pot, whether it was picking fights with neighbors or underlings (including his own sons) or needlessly alienating allies. In other words, the man made much of his own trouble.

ELEANOR OF AQUITAINE
Brood Mare to the Devil's Brood
(A.D. 1122–1204)

I advise you, King, to beware your wife and sons.

—*Count Raymond of Toulouse to King Henry II of England*

Every inch a match for her formidable husband, Henry II of England, Eleanor of Aquitaine not only bore him eight children (including both the famous Richard the Lion-Hearted, and the scurrilous John of England), she also outlived him by more than fifteen years, the same number of years in which he held her a virtual prisoner in Windsor Castle after she supported his sons in their rebellion against him in A.D. 1173. The fact that Eleanor outlived her husband by so many years is rendered all the more remarkable by the revelation that she was in fact twelve years older than her famous husband and had already borne two children by her first marriage.

Too much woman for her first husband, Louis VII of France, Eleanor found her match at age thirty in eighteen-year-old Henry Fitzempress, at the time duke of Normandy (and soon afterward king of England). Whether or not this second marriage was a love match, there can be no question that the couple shared a whole lot of passion. The two had eight children, seven of whom survived into adulthood, the so-called "Devil's Brood."

Not above using her children to play politics, Eleanor was an independent landowner (Aquitaine and Poitou) who acted like one, and constantly played her quarrelsome sons off against each other and against their own father. Tossed into prison at Windsor Castle after supporting her sons in their uprising against her husband, Eleanor waited Henry out: outliving him and seeing her favorite child (Richard) crowned king in his succession after Henry's death in A.D. 1189. She had been a prisoner for fifteen years at that point.

Living well into the reign of her last son John, Eleanor never really stopped doing her best to influence court politics, and never really retired from public life. Still feisty into her seventies, she personally ruled Aquitaine and Poitou as her personal fiefs until shortly before her death in A.D. 1204.

***

BASTARD ON CRUSADE

Originally married to King Louis VII of France, Eleanor accompanied him when he went to the Holy Land on crusade in A.D. 1146. While there she supposedly went a little wild. A later chronicler dutifully said of her purported antics: "Some say King Lewis [sic] carried her into the Holy Land, where she carried herself not very holily, but led a licentious life; and, which is the worst kind of licentiousness, in carnal familiarity with a Turk."

Was this true? Probably not. Such behavior on the part of any medieval French noblewoman would likely have resulted in her either being killed outright or divorced, stripped of her titles and property, and slapped into a convent for her troubles. That said, the royal couple squabbled constantly, with the result that they left the Holy Land and returned home by separate routes, and agreed to annul their marriage soon afterward.

★77★
HENRY THE YOUNG KING OF ENGLAND
Who Wants to Rule When There's Jousting to Be Done?
(A.D. 1155–1183)

Henry the son of the king of England, leaving the kingdom, passed three years in French contests and lavish expenditure.
—*Medieval chronicler Ralph of Diceto, archdeacon of Middlesex*

The subject of many troubadour songs idealizing the shining young knight in the golden age of chivalry, Henry the Young King, second son of Henry II of England and Eleanor of Aquitaine, was tall, handsome, charismatic, an enthusiastic jouster, and generous to his followers. Raised up to be "junior king" to his father at the age of fifteen (a symbolic gesture intended to secure his succession), Henry the Young King was everything the troubadours sang of him and more: stupid, shallow, vain, profligate, and utterly unsuited to run a tennis tournament, let alone a kingdom.

For all of his enthusiasm for jousting, Henry wasn't really any good at that, either. His mediocrity in the lists was directly related to his short attention span and inability to focus on anything long enough to master it. Even having the most famous knight in Christendom assigned to mentor him did no good. Sir William Marshall, who went on to serve as regent for King John's son Henry III, was a young knight of enormous repute whom Henry II set to teach his son how to fight in tournaments. Henry the Young King grew bored, though, never practiced, and wasn't interested in the hard work associated with mastering the arts of war.

In A.D. 1173, Henry joined his brothers (Richard, Geoffrey, and John) in rising in open revolt against their father. In this they were backed by their mother, the formidable Eleanor of Aquitaine, who found herself under house arrest for the rest of her husband's life for her trouble. At first it looked as if Henry was going to have to give away his kingdom piecemeal to his restive sons, but he had the money and the will to use it to pay mercenaries to fight in his name, and after a short time he prevailed.

$$\sim$$

BASTARD SHOWN UP BY A MARSHALL

Flanders (modern Belgium) during the late twelfth century was a hotbed of jousting tournaments, and Henry the Young King frequently deserted his duties as duke of neighboring Normandy to slip over to Flanders and enter a tournament or two. One particular time Henry and his entire retinue (including the by-then famous Sir William Marshall) stayed in a certain Flemish town where the king ran up enormous debts without having the money with him to make good. When the townspeople heard this, they locked their gates and guarded their town walls, determined not to allow the Young King to leave until he'd settled his accounts with them. His promises were not heeded. Apparently Henry the Young King was as free with his word as he was with other people's money. In stepped William Marshall, who offered his own word, vouching for the repayment of the Young King's debts. That was enough to satisfy the Flemings, who allowed the mortified Young King and his party to leave immediately.

By A.D. 1183, the Young King had still learned nothing about the right and wrong way to get what you want. Constantly demanding more authority from his father, he never demonstrated the slightest interest in showing the accountability and work ethic to go with it. Henry turned on his brother Richard, and invaded his duchy of Aquitaine. Instead of taking Richard by surprise, Henry took a beating, having his mercenaries defeated in battle and coming down with dysentery himself shortly after looting a monastery in order to be able to pay his men. Quickly realizing he was dying, Henry sent word for his father to come to his deathbed to exchange forgiveness with him, as was accepted Christian practice.

Henry II stayed away, afraid of a trap.

Kinda says it all, doesn't it?

★78★
RICHARD I THE LION-HEARTED
A Talent for War
(A.D. 1157–1199)

[Richard] cared for no success that was not reached by a path cut by his own sword and stained with the blood of his adversaries.

—*Medieval chronicler Gerald of Wales, archdeacon of Brecon*

The foremost example of what French troubadours called "le chevalier sans peur et sans reproche" ("the knight without fear and above reproach"), Richard Plantagenet, third son of Henry II of England and Eleanor of Aquitaine, has gotten a bad rap from recent historians looking to balance the portrait of him painted by contemporary chroniclers and expanded upon in the millennium since his death. But there is no changing the fact that Richard was the greatest strategist and one of the most fearless warriors of the Middle Ages, while also being eminently more honorable and trustworthy than any of his brothers, his father, mother, or other royal contemporaries.

His mother's favorite, Richard spent barely a year total in England during his ten-year reign. And yet he was remembered as "good king Richard," because he was a hell of a lot better ruler than anyone else looking to fill the job.

That said, he really loved war. And when the situation called for it, he could be the most ruthless of bastards, as evidenced by his slaughter of thousands of captives at one fell stroke during a siege in the Holy Land.

Having recently taken the city of Acre in the Holy Land, Richard found himself in a ticklish situation in late summer of A.D. 1191. While negotiating with the great Arab leader Saladin for surrender of various lands surrounding the city in exchange for the release of Muslim soldiers who had made up the garrison at Acre, the English king managed to alienate several allies, including his old rival King Philip Augustus of France and Archduke Leopold V of Austria (who later famously took revenge on Richard by holding him hostage for a huge ransom). Now facing an Arab army alone and eager to move his troops south to link up with other crusader forces in and around Jerusalem, Richard was growing impatient over the negotiations, while Saladin, hoping to neutralize Richard for the remainder of the campaign season, clearly dragged his feet.

GAY BASTARD?

Everyone who has seen the play or the film *The Lion in Winter* knows of the rumors of Richard's homosexuality: not much expressed interest in women, married only after becoming king, and never produced an heir, the medieval equivalent of the guy who's a jock in part because he likes to hang out with guys just a little too much. But modern scholarship has pretty much put the lie to this tale, especially in light of the fact that a supposed secret such as this one would have spread like wildfire among such gossipy medieval chroniclers as the monk Gerald of Wales had even a hint of it gotten out. In reality, Richard's wife Berengaria was likely barren, where Richard himself produced at least one verifiable bastard (later lord of Cognac) and rumors of another named Fulk.

In a move that modern readers find astonishing but which barely raised an eyebrow at the time, Richard marched all 2,700 members of the captured garrison of Acre outside the city gates and had them butchered by his troops in front of the eyes of the horrified Saladin and his soldiers. No longer tied by the need to guard his prisoners, Richard moved south and attacked Saladin's troops again at the battle of Arsuf a month later. He followed up this success by seeing his own nephew crowned king of Jerusalem.

While massacres of the type described above were fairly commonplace (Saladin had killed many more prisoners taken in the Arab victory over the crusaders at Hattin years earlier), the massacre at Acre has come down through history as a stain on the reputation of Richard the Lion-Hearted. People like their heroes to be clean morally, uncompromised, and decidedly unbastardly.

★79★
POPE INNOCENT III
Don't Let the Name Fool Ya
(CA. A.D. 1160–1216)

Use against heretics the spiritual sword of excommunication,
and if this does not prove effective, use the material sword.
—*Pope Innocent III*

Notwithstanding the name he took as pope, there was nothing innocent about the man born Lotario dei Conti. A powerbroker in church circles for a decade before he assumed the shoes of the fisherman at age thirty-eight in A.D. 1198, Innocent III proved one of the most ruthless and effective of medieval popes, a far cry from such bumblers and dilettantes as Stephen VI and Benedict IX. And yet in his treatment of heretics and in his efforts to launch the Fourth Crusade, Innocent showed himself to be an unmitigated bastard.

To begin with, Innocent was one of those most dangerous of men: a religious zealot. And he was big on signs from God. As a result, he accepted his election as just such a sign from the guy upstairs that the Church needed protecting (from external enemies) and cleansing (to deal with internal enemies). In other words, Innocent III looked around him and saw nothing but foes.

The result was a couple of holy wars: the Fourth Crusade, launched in A.D. 1198 and intended to retrieve the Holy Land from Muslim nonbelievers (enemies without) and the Albigensian Crusade, launched against practitioners of the Cathar heresy (Christians who did not accept the rule of the papacy and had other dangerous ideas about Jesus, his mother, and, of course, God).

Innocent's call for a crusade to free the Holy Land resulted in a bloody invasion of Palestine, and also led directly to the sack of Constantinople (whose residents were Orthodox Christians). Leaving out the havoc this crusade wreaked on the Muslim and Jewish occupants of Palestine (who didn't count to Christians in that day and age), the pope was horrified by what happened next: the murder and rape of tens of thousands of the city's Christian residents. Apparently it hadn't occurred to him that some of the knights who answered his call to arms would regard Orthodox Christians as enemies.

Innocent's conflict with the Cathars of southern France, on the other hand, left no such bad taste in his mouth. In A.D. 1208, a representative the pope had sent to negotiate with the nobles giving protection to these heretics wound up murdered. Innocent's response was swift and brutal. Any person making war on these Cathars, he said, was entitled to their property; furthermore, he said, any Catholic allowing Cathars to live among them unmolested was no good Catholic, and their lives and property ought to also be forfeited.

The result?

Tens of thousands killed over the following twenty-year period, and the rich culture of southern France completely destroyed.

But Innocent didn't live to see any of this. He died suddenly in A.D. 1216, his last crusade still incomplete.

BASTARD IN HIS OWN WORDS

[I]t grieves us most of all that, against the orthodox faith, there are now arising more . . . ministers of diabolical error who are ensnaring the souls of the simple and ruining them. . . . You shall exercise the rigor of the ecclesiastical power against them and all those who have made themselves suspected by associating with them. They may not appeal from your judgments, and if necessary, you may cause the princes and people to suppress them with the sword.

★80★
GEOFFREY II OF BRITTANY
"That Son of Perdition"
(A.D. 1158–1186)

[O]verflowing with words, soft as oil, possessed, by his syrupy and persuasive eloquence, of the power of dissolving the seemingly indissoluble, able to corrupt two kingdoms with his tongue; of tireless endeavour, a hypocrite and a dissembler.
—*Gerald of Wales, archdeacon of Brecon*

If ever there was a prototypical schemer, it was Geoffrey Plantagenet, the fourth son of Henry II of England and his wife, Eleanor of Aquitaine. According to our sources, this duke of Brittany's only saving grace was his charm.

Henry II had the dubious distinction of inspiring very little loyalty in his sons—as denoted by the fact that all four of the ones who survived to adulthood seem to have been constantly either plotting against him or actually at war with him (and with each other). And the worst among this "Devil's Brood" was his fourth son, Geoffrey.

Geoffrey started out his career as a bastard early, joining a rebellion against his father before his sixteenth birthday. It would not be the last time he intrigued against the old king, and his most frequent dance partner in this sort of treason was not one of his brothers but the duplicitous son of his mother's first husband, Philip Augustus, the king of France.

In fact, the two men were so close that Philip appointed Geoffrey his seneschal, a court official of immense power, acting as the king's personal representative in instances when the king himself was absent.

But it's not as if either man was the other's puppet. They were both constantly scheming (there's that word again) for personal gain; in Geoffrey's case, he was looking to expand his power base from the duchy of Brittany (he had received it as a wedding present when he married the heir of the previous duke in A.D. 1181), usually at the expense of either his father or his brothers. Geoffrey literally went to war with a relative no less than twenty times during the last ten years of his life.

In the end, all of his machinations served him not one whit. Geoffrey died young, aged just twenty-seven, at the court of his close friend and benefactor, Philip Augustus. Accounts vary as to the cause of his death, but he most likely died after being trampled during a joust.

According to several eyewitnesses, Philip was so grief-stricken by Geoffrey's death that he tried to jump into the casket with Geoffrey at the duke's funeral.

Whether anyone else mourned the arch-schemer's passing is not recorded.

IRRELIGIOUS BASTARD

Truly one of the "Devil's Brood," Geoffrey had a novel way of covering his expenses when he found himself short of cash (which he often did). He would simply find and loot the closest church property, be it monastery, abbey, or simple parish church. It didn't much matter to him whether the clerical establishment he was currently treating as the medieval equivalent of an ATM was on his land or on that of another lord. To Geoffrey, they were all fair game. Worst still, he seems to have truly relished the prospect of looting churches. Small wonder that his contemporaries among church chroniclers are unanimous in their disdain for this particular Plantagenet!

★81★
JOHN I OF ENGLAND
Short, Miserly, and Mean
(A.D. 1167–1216)

After King John had captured Arthur [duke of Brittany and John's nephew] and kept him alive in prison for some time, at length, in the castle of Rouen, after dinner on the Thursday before Easter, when he was drunk and possessed by the devil, he slew him with his own hand and, tying a heavy stone to the body, cast it into the Seine. It was discovered by a fisherman in his net and, being dragged to the shore and recognised, was taken for secret burial in fear of the tyrant, to the priory of Bec called Notre Dame des Pres.
—Annals of the Abbey of Margam

The youngest of the so-called "Devil's Brood," and certainly the least among the sons of Henry II, John Plantagenet has come down through history with a well-deserved reputation for venality, cowardice, treachery, and vanity. The legendary near-comic foil of the mythical outlaw Robin Hood, the truth about John Lackland (as he was called while still a young prince) is far darker than the legend. Because in the final accounting there was nothing comic about the vicious little bastard known to history as King John of England.

Despite his flaws, John was, for some strange reason, his father's favorite, even after he joined Henry's other sons in rebellion while still a teenager.

By all measures except one, John was a failure as a monarch and as a man. While ruling in his brother Richard's name while Richard was on crusade, he stripped the kingdom bare, supposedly to pay Richard's ransom after he'd been taken captive by the duke of Austria. (John kept the money.)

185

After Richard's death, once he became king and ruler of the so-called "Angevin Empire," which encompassed not just England and Ireland but all of western France, John found himself outmaneuvered time and again by the crafty King Philip Augustus of France, with the result that through a combination of war and diplomacy Philip stripped him of most of his French possessions, including the all-important duchy of Normandy. The result was that John died with far fewer French possessions than any English king since William the Conqueror crossed the Channel in A.D. 1066.

CRUEL BASTARD

John enjoyed seeing people suffer but lacked the fortitude to do it himself (except when dead drunk, as in the example quoted above). He favored starving those who displeased him to death, as was the case of Maud of Saint-Valery and her son, whom he locked up in the dungeon of their own castle. But his cruelty didn't stop there: stories of the ingenious tortures he inflicted on his subjects and his enemies include tales of people roasted alive, blinded with vinegar, and hung by the thumbs. One old goat, a self-styled prophet named Peter of Wakefield, foolishly prophesied that John would not be king after the next anniversary of his ascension. When John got wind of this, he had the man thrown into prison until after Ascension Day had passed, then dragged him behind a horse for several miles and had him hanged. Then he turned around and did the same thing to Peter's son!

The one area where John was successful where most of his brothers failed was in siring children. He had at least five legitimate children and twelve acknowledged bastards.

His greatest failure might also have been his greatest gift to future generations of subjects. In order to pay for his many pointless wars in France, John had bled the country dry. And since he had targeted the Church in these depredations as well, he had no backing when a group of nobles rose against him and forced the concessions that became known as the Magna Carta, an important step in the establishment of democracy, shortly before his death in A.D. 1215.

Talk about the law of unintended consequences!

PHILIP II AUGUSTUS OF FRANCE
Cowardly, Duplicitous, and Effective
(A.D. 1165–1223)

> By the grace of God there is born to us this night a King who
> shall be a hammer to the English.
> —*Member of the Parisian mob (attr. Gerald of Wales)*

Born in A.D. 1165 to the ailing French king Louis VII, Philip was crowned king at age fifteen after his father suffered a stroke and began to lose his mental faculties. Louis had been a good man, and a lousy king. His son, clever, cowardly, and calculating, would prove a lousy man and a good king.

Philip did more to strengthen the French crown and expand its power than any other king since Charlemagne. And he did it in large part by destroying the wide-ranging holdings of fellow royal bastard Henry II of England and his quarrelsome bastard sons. Furthermore, he did it by playing them off against each other. Forming close personal friendships with each of Henry's sons, he supported them in their frequent rebellions against their father.

Initially, relations between Philip and Henry's son Richard were good—but they soured. The two went on crusade together in the Holy Land, then began to squabble over who was running the show in their combined military campaigns. Tensions rose. Philip was touchy because he was a physical coward who eschewed most forms of combat. Plus, he saw an opportunity to peel off more of Richard's properties in northern France while Richard was distracted by crusading in the Holy Land. Claiming that he was needed at home, Philip made ready to withdraw. Richard's reply was scathing: "It is a shame and a disgrace on my lord if he goes away without having finished the business that brought him hither. But still, if he finds himself in bad health, or is afraid lest he should die here, his will be done."

Philip made him pay for the remark. While Richard was still in the Holy Land, Philip presented documents to Richard's representatives in Normandy, purporting to be from Richard and returning parts of northern France to the French crown. They were forgeries.

The two monarchs went to war soon afterward, and stayed at war until Richard's death in A.D. 1199.

Once the incompetent John succeeded his brother, Philip managed to reverse the roles the two men's fathers had played: he outwitted the dimwitted English king at every turn, just as Henry II had done with his own father decades earlier. This culminated in Philip's taking the duchy of Normandy from the English late in John's reign.

$$\sim$$

BASTARD BIGAMIST

Philip's first wife died young in childbirth, and in A.D. 1193, he took Ingeborg, the daughter of the king of Denmark, as his second wife. But Philip couldn't stand the sight of her. Setting her aside, he tried to get the marriage annulled on the grounds that they were too closely related by blood and that he hadn't consummated the marriage. Not bothering to wait for a dispensation from the pope, Philip married a third time, siring several children by his new wife, Agnes of Merania. But Ingeborg hung in there, refusing to concede that they hadn't sealed the wedding with sex. Eventually the pope agreed with her, and Philip was forced to accept her back as queen of France in A.D. 1213, by which time Agnes had died.

★83★
OTTO IV OF GERMANY
Stupid Is as Stupid Does
(A.D. 1165–1223)

—Physically large, with a much-noted resemblance to Richard the Lionheart, whose favorite he was, Otto was by common consent an unreliable braggart, a rather stupid, bungling, inefficient but arrogant man, who let his tongue run away with him and made lavish promises he had no intention of keeping.
—*Frank McLynn*, Richard & John: Kings at War

The son of Henry the Lion, duke of Bavaria and Saxony, and Matilda Plantagenet, this future Holy Roman Emperor was big, loud, handsome, and dumb. Raised in England by his grandfather, Otto was slated at various times to become earl of York and king (by marriage) of Scotland. Both ploys proved to be busts, so his favorite uncle Richard made him count of Poitou.

Otto looked the part of a king, even if he didn't possess much ability, and the Plantagenets had big dreams for him. So when Holy Roman Emperor Henry VI died in A.D. 1197, Richard I advanced Otto as a candidate to succeed him as both Holy Roman Emperor and king of Germany (in truth, there wasn't much difference between the two at that point), hoping to use Otto as a counterweight in his ongoing feud with the French king, Philip Augustus.

Nearly a decade of civil war in Germany followed, as Pope Innocent III backed first Otto, then one or the other of the two rival claimants of the throne.

When Philip of Swabia, the leading candidate for the throne of the Holy Roman Empire, was assassinated in A.D. 1208, the pope switched his allegiance to Otto. In exchange for the pope's backing, Otto offered him most of the imperial fiefs in Italy, plus the right to appoint all German bishops. Otto had no intention of actually honoring this promise, and once the pope had crowned him Holy Roman Emperor later that same year, he blithely ignored the pope's insistence on his new rights. Instead, he reconquered all of northern Italy and menaced the pope in Rome.

Enraged, Innocent (a fellow bastard, and not someone to be trifled with) excommunicated him the next year. This move signaled a shift in Otto's fortunes. Allied with his uncle John (the king of England) against the other contender for the throne, Frederick of Hohenstaufen (who was allied with Philip Augustus), Otto again invaded Italy, then turned northward, and with his uncle, got flattened in the Battle of Bouvines in A.D. 1214.

Finished politically, he limped off to his family's possessions in Brunswick to hide out and lick his wounds. He was deposed as both king of Germany and Holy Roman Emperor within a year. Three years afterward he died under mysterious circumstances.

———————————— ∽ ————————————

BASTARD'S DEMISE

Depending on which source you're reading, Otto either died of a drug overdose or was stricken by a debilitating illness (possibly dysentery) and begged the local abbot to help him purge himself of his sins in a most colorful manner: "deposed, dethroned, he was flung full length on the ground by the Abbot, confessing his sins, while the reluctant priests beat him bloodily to death. Such was the end of the first and last Welf Emperor."

★84★
HENRY III OF ENGLAND
A Saintly King with Locusts for Relatives
(A.D. 1207–1272)

> His mind seemed not to stand on a firm basis, for every sudden
> accident put him into passion.
>
> —*Anonymous contemporary account of Henry III*

In A.D. 1207, a son was born to King John of England, a baby boy who would grow up to be very little like his sour, saturnine father. Sweet-natured, pious Henry III (named for his grandfather, the restless, brilliant bastard Henry II) was generous to a fault, suffered from abandonment issues, and was easily manipulated by his French relatives. The one characteristic he shared with his father was that he was a disaster as a king.

Henry was, to put it bluntly, a bungler. Weak-willed and vacillating, he tended to follow the counsel of the last person in the room to give him a suggestion. To top it off, Henry never got over either the death of his father or his mother's literal abandonment of him while he was still a child. Constantly seeking approval and looking about for surrogate father figures, when he married, he allowed his wife's family (the Savoyards) to dominate his government, enriching themselves in the process.

Not to be outdone, Henry's half-brothers by his mother's second husband swooped down onto England once they were close to adulthood, hoping to cash in on the king's largesse. They were not disappointed. Henry showered his brothers with titles, property, and honors. He even managed to get one elected bishop of Winchester despite the fact that he was illiterate, still in his teens, and hadn't spent a day as a priest!

"The Lusignans" (as Henry's half-brothers and their followers were known, in recognition that they were the sons of Hugh of Lusignan) repaid Henry's largesse with repeated acts of violence towards their rivals, looting, pillaging, even killing neighbors, all while Henry turned an uncritical blind eye. This brought them in conflict with the Savoyard relatives of Henry's wife, and in turn with a confederation of nobles concerned with Henry's attempts to rewrite the Magna Carta, the document granting English subjects certain rights and privileges that Henry's father had signed under protest in A.D. 1215.

The result was two decades of bloody civil war. By A.D. 1265, the fighting had largely ceased, but Henry's grip on reality, never all that strong, began to lapse. In A.D. 1268, he had a bout of what can only be described as temporary insanity, renounced his Christian faith, and claimed to be a follower of the old Germanic gods Odin and Thor. A week later he came to his senses and proclaimed himself once again a Christian. He died five years later, succeeded by another, more capable bastard: his son, Edward Longshanks.

ORPHANED BASTARD

John died in A.D. 1216, leaving his nine-year-old son as king. In situations such as this, the queen mother usually served as regent, with nobles to help her rule in the underaged monarch's name. John's widow, Isabella of Angouleme, had no love for England, though, and four years after John's death left for France and a second marriage (to a French nobleman named Hugh of Lusignan), abandoning her young son as well as her adopted country in the process. For all intents and purposes the boy king was orphaned while barely into his teens.

★85★
EDWARD I OF ENGLAND
When the Only Tool You Have Is a Hammer, Use It on the Scots
(A.D. 1239–1307)

> Hic est Edwardvs Primus Scottorum Malleus (Latin for: "Here is Edward I, Hammer of the Scots").
>
> —*Edward I's epitaph, carved on his tomb in Westminster*

Psychologist Abraham Maslow once famously remarked, "When the only tool you have is a hammer, you tend to see every problem as a nail." He might easily have been talking about Edward I, king of England from A.D. 1273 to 1307. In Edward's case, the hammer was the employment of ruthless, overwhelming, all-consuming violence in order to solve his political problems.

Born in A.D. 1239, Edward was hobbled from early age with ill health. But where his father, Henry III, was weak-willed and vacillating, young Edward possessed deep resources of both will and fire (he had the so-called "Plantagenet temper"), and managed to make a full recovery.

His father's inability to rule coupled with his favoring foreign-born (in other words, French) sycophants over his "natural subjects" led to repeated clashes with his barons. Ironically enough, these nobles were led by the king's own brother-in-law, the foreign-born (yep, you guessed it, French) earl of Leicester, Simon de Montfort.

Forced by these circumstances to grow up quick (and at 6'2" he towered over most of his contemporaries, earning the nickname "Longshanks" because of his long legs), Edward quickly developed a reputation as a great warrior.

194

During the resulting civil war, Edward fought mostly on his father's side, and was even briefly a royal captive of Montfort and his allies. In A.D. 1265, A.D, the now twenty-six-year-old Edward, in command of his father's forces, trapped and killed Montfort and crushed his rebellion at the Battle of Lewes (in Sussex).

After securing victory at home, he went on crusade to the Holy Land (where he survived an assassination attempt in his tent by whacking his would-be killer in the head with a stool, then wresting the fellow's dagger from his grasp and using it on him). While there, he learned of his father's death and returned to England in A.D. 1273.

<hr>

BASTARD OF WALES

When Edward took the throne in A.D. 1273, he immediately inherited a conflict with the semi-independent principality of Wales on England's western border. Llewellyn Ap Gryffudd (pronounced "Griffith"), the hereditary prince of Wales, clashed with Edward many times over the years before the prince was finally defeated and killed in battle in A.D. 1282. Afterward, his severed head was sent to Edward as a grim trophy of the successful pacification of Wales. The heir to the English throne has borne the title "Prince of Wales" ever since.

<hr>

As king, Edward set about pacifying neighboring Wales, England's Irish possessions, and pressing his own claim to the Scottish throne. For the next three decades, he was continually at war with his neighbors: building a line of castles on the Welsh marches; invading Scotland time and again; and everywhere Edward went, blood, pestilence, and famine followed him. In one instance, at Berwick-Upon-Tweed, Edward was so enraged by the resistance of the townspeople that when his forces finally took the city, he ordered the entire population slaughtered.

He didn't limit his bloodlust to conquered neighbors. Before he expelled the Jews from his kingdom in A.D. 1290, he imprisoned their leaders, hanging 300 of them for no other offense than being Jewish!

Edward even seized the legendary Stone of Scone, an ancient chunk of rock on which Scottish kings had been crowned since prehistoric times (the Scots would not get the stone back until the twentieth century). By this time, the Scottish king was nothing more than the English king's puppet. Under Edward's reign, Wales and Ireland were also completely subjugated for the first time.

No wonder when the great man died, his son had carved on his funeral slab "The Hammer of the Scots." What the Scots thought of this is not exactly printable.

★86★
PHILIP IV THE FAIR
OF FRANCE
Don't Let The Name Fool Ya, Redux
(A.D. 1268–1314)

The current occupant is unfit to sit on the throne of Peter.
—*Philip IV of France*

Philip IV inherited a kingdom beyond broke: his father and grandfather had bankrupted the realm with a series of expensive wars of conquest (including crusades to the Holy Land, for which effort and expenditure the French had exactly nothing to show).

In short order, he turned on those to whom he owed the most money (Jewish moneylenders and the banking house of the Order of the Knights Templar), driving out the Jews and destroying the Templars. Then he insisted on taxing those who had previously enjoyed tax-exempt status— the French possessions of the Catholic Church. This in turn brought the French king into conflict with the papacy, with a surprising result.

Coming to the throne at the age of seventeen in A.D. 1285, Philip tallied what he owed and what was owed him, realized he was in hock to a lot of different people, and promptly set about wringing as much money as he could out of the kingdom's Jewish residents. After forcing a ruinous special tax on them from A.D. 1291 until 1303, by which time he'd bankrupted most of the Jews still living in France, he expelled them from the kingdom.

Then he turned on the Templars.

These crusader knights had paid the massive ransom that got Philip's grandfather Louis IX released from Egyptian captivity in A.D. 1254. In the decades since, the interest on this loan had continued to accrue. Exempt from taxation and in position to lend and pass along money (like a medieval Western Union), the Templars were loaded and ripe for the picking.

Rather than make even interest payments on this loan, Philip laid plans, then in A.D. 1307, seized Jacques de Molay, the Grand Master, and most of the leadership of the order, accusing them of heresy, and torturing confessions out of most of them.

The result? These proceedings gave Philip legal cover to seize the holdings of the Templar bank and use them to pay his debts. Plus, with the order itself destroyed, there was no one to enforce payment of his own massive debt to the Templars!

And then there was the papacy.

Philip insisted on taxing the Church, a move that pissed off the current pope, Boniface VIII, who issued instructions in A.D. 1302 forbidding the French church from paying the tax. When Philip got hold of these instructions, he publicly burned them. Trying the pope in absentia, he questioned his fitness to be pontiff. Moving quickly, he sent French troops to arrest the pope, who died shortly afterward (partly of humiliation). Then he insisted on getting one of his close associates in the French church elected pope, as Clement V. (More on him in Chapter 87.)

Philip IV died in a hunting accident in A.D. 1314, leaving a far more balanced budget than the one he'd inherited. But at what cost in blood and good will?

------------------------------ ✑ ------------------------------

WHAT'S IN A NAME?

A very handsome, light-haired, blue-eyed man, Philip was known as "le Bel" during his lifetime. This translated as "the Fair," but as in "fair-skinned," not as in "fair-minded." No one who know him would have called Philip a fair-minded person.

★87★
POPE CLEMENT V
The Man Who Hijacked the Papacy
(A.D. 1264–1314)

for after him will come, in deeds more foul,
a lawless shepherd from the west, to trim
the two of us and move us down this hole.
Another Jason will he be, like him
We read of in the book of Maccabees,
Who'll bend the king of France to suit his whim.
—*Dante Alleghieri*, The Inferno

Raymond Bertrand de Gouth was bought and paid for by the king of France long before he became pope, and he remained the king's man after being elevated to the papacy in A.D. 1303. He helped Philip IV suppress the order of the Knights Templar and steal their wealth, then agreed to hijack the papacy and move it from Rome (where the mob was rioting daily calling for an Italian pope) to Avignon, where no one would dare riot against either the French pope or the French king!

The reason there was an opening in the papacy was because the previous pope (Benedict IX, for those keeping score at home) had been poisoned by agents of the French king. And before him, Pope Boniface VIII had also been murdered (beaten and left to die of his injuries) by the very same thugs, led by Philip IV's ruthless hatchet man, William of Nogaret.

In debt to Philip IV of France (who had backed him in his bid for the papacy) who was in turn in debt to the Knights Templar, Clement played ball from the day he was crowned pontiff in Lyon (afraid to go to Rome to be crowned because of the threat of murder at the hands of an increasingly anti-French Roman mob).

Within two years, the Templars had been charged with heresy; their order disbanded by papal decree; their leaders tortured into confessions of bizarre, heretical rituals; their lands, cash, and other property seized—all with Clement's blessing. In fact, only the pope could have so thoroughly destroyed a holy order such as the Templars, because they served at the pleasure of the pope.

With the Templar corpse barely cold, Clement, still fearful of setting foot in Italy, set up shop in a couple of different locations in southern France, eventually settling on Avignon as the perfect place for his new court. He never returned to Rome during his lifetime, and the papacy stayed in Avignon for seventy years.

In A.D. 1314, the last Grand Master of the Knights Templar, Jacques de Molay, was burned at the stake as a heretic, after nearly seven years in prison. He is alleged to have died with a curse on his lips intended for the two men most responsible for the recent reversal of fortune for himself and his order: Clement V and Philip IV. If this is true, then he got his dying wish. Both men were dead within months of his own expiration, an interesting riff on the whole notion of damnatio memoriae ("damnation of memory").

PACKING THE COLLEGE

One of the first things Clement V did after being confirmed as pontiff was to create nine new cardinal seats and fill them all with Frenchmen. By doing this he not only outraged many of the other cardinals but also ensured that the papacy would stay both in French hands and in France itself for the next seventy years.

★88★
KING EDWARD II OF ENGLAND
Giving Away the Kingdom to His Boyfriends
(A.D. 1284–1327)

You baseborn whoreson! Now you want to give lands away—you who have never gained any? As the Lord lives, were it not for fear of breaking up the kingdom, you should never enjoy your inheritance!
—*King Edward I of England to his son, Edward, Prince of Wales (later Edward II)*

In the bit of conversation quoted above, the person being called a prostitute's progeny (as much of an insult in the fourteenth century as it is today) was the king's own progeny, his eldest son and later successor, Edward II.

When it came to both the character and fitness to rule of his son and heir, Edward Longshanks was not only colorful, he was accurate.

The elder Edward had come taken the throne with an act of signal violence and then employed violence as a catchall solution to any number of problems both foreign and domestic. The example he set for his son was fearsome, decisive, and warlike.

And his son Edward of Caernarvon was nothing like him.

Where Longshanks was grimly competent, plainspoken, and blunt, the younger Edward was flowery, handsome, well-groomed, and ineffectual. Where Longshanks valued no one's counsel so much as his own, his son was easily influenced by his retinue of hangers-on.

Edward I had grown up in the shadow of a weak father who also was a bad king. In attempting to be a stronger father figure to his own son and heir, he wound up producing a successor with more in common with his incompetent grandfather (Henry III) than with his force-of-nature father.

Oh, and Edward II was gay.

Definitely a cross to bear in thirteenth-century England, Edward made the situation all the worse by not bothering to worry what his subjects might think of his publicly treating his closest friends more like lovers than as boon companions.

The genuine problem wasn't the king's predilection for other men. It was his predilection for other men on whom he spent lavishly, heaping titles and cash and lands on them as a sign of both his largesse and his favor. And for their part, pretty boys like Piers Gaveston and Hugh le Despenser eagerly soaked up what the king gave away.

It couldn't last.

Within five years, Edward II had bankrupted the kingdom with his spending. His nobles restless, his queen completely fed up with him, something had to give. By A.D. 1326, Edward's time had run out. His wife, Isabella (daughter of the king of France), had gone to France ostensibly on a diplomatic mission, only to return at the head of a mercenary army. She challenged Edward for his throne, all in the name of their underage son.

A couple of quick battles later, and Edward was soundly defeated, captured, and thrown into prison. Within a month, he had been secretly executed in one of the most barbaric manners imaginable.

——————————————— ⟋⟍ ———————————————

END OF A BASTARD

Because the killing of a king was seen as both a sin and an act of treason, Edward was murdered in a way that made it look as if he'd died of natural causes. His killers pushed a red-hot soldering iron into the king's body through his anus. It left not a mark on him to show the agony in which he had died.

★89★

ROGER MORTIMER, EARL OF MARCH

Screwing the Queen Doesn't Make You King

(A.D. 1287–1330)

The King of Folly.

—*Sir Geoffrey Mortimer, son of Roger Mortimer, about his father*

Roger Mortimer came of age during a violent time in a violent place (the Anglo-Welsh borderlands), serving a prince (Edward II) who seemed in many ways his opposite: effete, capricious, soft. Fostered into the royal household while still in his teens after the death of his father, Mortimer saw firsthand how Edward indulged handsome favorites such as Piers Gaveston (who was briefly Mortimer's guardian).

When Edward appropriated some of the Mortimer family lands in order to make a gift of them to another of his favorites (Edward le Despenser), Mortimer rose in opposition to the king, lost in battle, and was thrown into the Tower of London for a time. Escaping by drugging his jailer, he fled the kingdom and went into exile in France.

It was while in exile in France that Mortimer became first acquainted with, and then attached to, Isabella, princess of France, and Edward's queen. Ostensibly in France on a diplomatic mission, but really there because she had grown fed up with her husband, Isabella made common cause with the energetic, forceful Mortimer. In no time the two were lovers, planning to take the kingdom from her husband.

Invading England in A.D. 1326 at the head of an army of Flemish mercenaries, the two were joined by locals, including the people of London and the earl of Lancaster. After a couple of minor battles, the deposed King Edward fled to the west, wandering in Wales before eventually surrendering to the two in return for his life being spared.

It turned out he got a bad deal.

De facto ruler of England for three years (A.D. 1327–1330), Mortimer had honors heaped upon him, swaggered around, pissing off the wrong people, and alienating the young king Edward III, for whom he was ostensibly regent. It couldn't last.

In A.D. 1330, Edward seized power. While his own mother could expect mercy at his hands, Mortimer received none. He was hanged at Tyburn Hill that same year for treason and exercising royal power without authority.

∽

GRUESOME BASTARD

It is widely believed to have been Roger Mortimer's idea to kill Edward II by shoving a red-hot poker up his ass, thereby leaving no mark on his body to indicate foul play, while also making sly reference to the deposed king's "buggery" with his favorites.

★90★
PEDRO THE CRUEL OF CASTILE
The Nickname Says It All
(A.D. 1334–1369)

> We must add likewise that this Don Pedro, king of Castile, who at present is driven out of his realm, is a man of great pride, very cruel, and full of bad dispositions. The kingdom of Castile has suffered many grievances at his hands: many valiant men have been beheaded and murdered, without justice or reason, so that these wicked actions, which he ordered or consented to, he owes the loss of his kingdom.
>
> —*Medieval chronicler Jean Froissart,* Chronicles

A bigamous, vicious monster, Pedro of Castile was king from A.D. 1350 to 1369. He probably wouldn't have lasted that long had he not been propped up late in his reign by one of the great military minds of his age, his son-in-law, John of Gaunt, Duke of Lancaster.

Neither much of a leader nor much of a soldier, the best that could be said of Pedro was that he wasn't as anti-Semitic as the rest of the rulers of the Iberian Peninsula. In fact, his most consistent supporters during his years as king were the Jews of such large cities as Seville.

But Pedro was also capricious, destructive, and completely indifferent to human suffering. Even his generosity came at a price.

Pedro was very grateful to his son-in-law Edward the Black (prince of England) for working so hard to help him hold on to his crown. He showed his gratitude in many ways, including the bestowing of large gifts on his son-in-law. Among these was a huge jewel that eventually found its way into the crown of current English monarch Elizabeth II. He got the jewel from a guest in his palace the Alcazar—a guest he killed in order to steal it.

This wasn't Pedro the Cruel's last murder. Far from it. Once while walking the streets of Seville, he killed a man he didn't even know simply because he didn't like the way the man looked at him. When the time came for Pedro to pay for these murders (because hey, even the king isn't above the law), he had an effigy of himself made in stone, then put it on trial before him, and then he (the king) passed sentence on himself (in effigy) and had himself (in effigy) beheaded, with the head (again, of the effigy) to be placed at the spot where the murder had taken place. It can be seen there to this day.

Fancying himself quite the womanizer, Pedro made molesting women something of a hobby. One woman who rejected him was burned alive on his orders for the transgression of saying no to a king. He even had his own wife murdered—by arrow shot. One woman burned her face with acid so that the rutting king wouldn't find her so attractive.

Unlike other vicious bastards in this book, Pedro's story doesn't end with him dying of old age, unpunished for his many crimes. Instead, it ends with him being captured in battle by the forces of his rival, Henry of Trastamara. He was beheaded on the spot. Truly a fitting end for a deserving bastard!.

———————————— ✍ ————————————

BIGAMOUS BASTARD

Pedro secretly married a noblewoman named Maria de Padilla in A.D. 1353. This became a problem when his family arranged for him to wed Blanche of Bourbon later that same year. When confronted with accusations that he had already married Padilla, Pedro did what any bastard would do: He lied. After three days, he abandoned his second wife and gave up all pretense of not being involved with Padilla. The couple eventually had four children together. As for the unfortunate Blanche, she was murdered by crossbow bolt (on Pedro's command).

BERNABÒ VISCONTI, LORD OF MILAN

Why Let Brotherhood Stand in the Way of Your Territorial Ambitions?

(A.D. 1323–1385)

The count de Vertus, whose name was John Galeas Visconti, and his uncle were the greatest personages in all Lombardy. Sir Galeas and sir Bernabo were brothers, and had peaceably reigned and governed that country. One of these lords possessed nine cities, and the other ten; the city of Milan was under their government alternately, one year each. When sir Galeas, the father of the count de Vertus, died, the affections of the uncle for his nephew were much weakened; and sir Galeas suspected, that now his father was dead, his uncle Bernabo would seize his lordships, in like manner as sir Galeas, his father, and uncle Bernabo had done to their brother sir Matthew, whom they had put to death.

—*Jean Froissart,* Chronicles

Scion of a family that had ruled Milan for well over one hundred years (off and on) by the time he was born, Bernabò Visconti was an energetic ruler, first with his two brothers, then with one, and finally by himself (A.D. 1378–1385), until giving way to his nephew Gian Galeazzo, the greatest of the Visconti rulers of Milan. He was also a fratricidal despot who taxed the residents of Milan into poverty in order to bankroll the incessant wars he fought with a series of popes and rival cities such as Venice and Verona, all in an attempt to make himself master of northern Italy.

Capable of great charm when it suited him, Bernabò was also notorious for his ironic cruelty. At one point excommunicated by the pope, Bernabò received the two papal emissaries who brought the fancy order of excommunication (parchment embossed with a lead seal and tied with a silken cord), listened as they read the documents aloud, and when they tried to present the document, had them seized and held until they ate the order, parchment, seal, cord, and all!

Before his brother died, the two men devised a particularly sadistic form of torture that mimicked portions of the Bible, lasting up to forty days. Not surprisingly, most of their victims died within the first few days.

After his brother Galeazzo's death in A.D. 1378, Bernabò ruled alone, freezing out his nephew Gian Galeazzo. Fearing that Bernabò might poison him as he had his own elder brother (see sidebar), Gian Galeazzo caught Bernabò unsuspecting, traveling between cities with a light escort, seized his uncle, and threw him in prison. Then, in an ironic echo of Bernabò's own actions with his brother Matteo, Gian Galeazzo had his uncle poisoned.

Bunch of poisonous bastards!

——————————— ༄ ———————————

BASTARD BROTHERS

Bernabò initially shared power with his two brothers, Matteo and Galeazzo. But where Galeazzo, a patron of the early Renaissance poet Petrarch, was intelligent, educated, and cultured, Matteo was another matter entirely. The eldest and roughest of the three brothers, Matteo possessed all the viciousness for which the Visconti were notorious, and none of the ability they also possessed (especially their talent for governing). Increasingly a liability to the two other brothers (they were supposed to alternate ruling Milan every year, in a three-year rotation), Matteo was murdered at a feast in A.D. 1355, poisoned by his own brothers. Ruthless bastards!

★92★
CHARLES THE BAD, KING OF NAVARRE
The Nickname Says It All, Redux
(A.D. 1332–1387)

In the year of the sea-battle off Winchelsea, Philip VI of France died and was succeeded by John II, 'the Good'. Though there was a temporary lull in the war with England, the new King's internal difficulties were soon increased by the intrigues of his cousin, Charles 'the Bad', King of Navarre, who had rival claims to the French throne. Early in 1356 Charles of Navarre was seized and put in prison, but his family and the vassals of his fiefs in Normandy continued to give trouble, in alliance with the English.

—*Jean Froissart*, Chronicles

The king of Navarre (a small kingdom in the Pyrenees Mountains split between modern-day southern France and northern Spain), Charles II ("le Mauvais": "the Bad") married the daughter of his rival John II ("le Bon": "the Good"), king of France, and intrigued against him for the rest of his life. A schemer and malcontent, Charles changed sides in the Hundred Years' War between England and France more times than an obsessive-compulsive changes socks. Using Navarre the way William the Conqueror used England (as a source of revenue), Charles plotted to kill the king of France, and succeeded in having his top government official murdered, then went on to suffer a gruesome death of his own.

Initially an enthusiastic supporter of John the Good (he served as his autho-rized lieutenant in several campaigns and married his daughter), Charles was livid when in A.D. 1353, John gave the fiefdoms of Angoulême, Brie, and Champagne to his constable Charles de la Cerda (known generally as "Charles of Spain"). Our Charles (the bad one) believed the territories belonged to him, as they had been taken from his mother by previous French kings, with very little in the way of compensation. He ended up picking a quarrel with Charles of Spain.

——————————————— ༄ ———————————————

DEATH OF A BASTARD

Charles died in a grotesque manner later described in lurid detail by medieval chronicler Francis Blagdon: "Charles the Bad, having fallen into such a state of decay that he could not make use of his limbs, consulted his physician, who ordered him to be wrapped up from head to foot, in a linen cloth impregnated with brandy, so that he might be inclosed (sic) in it to the very neck as in a sack. It was night when this remedy was administered. One of the female attendants of the palace, charged to sew up the cloth that contained the patient, having come to the neck, the fixed point where she was to finish her seam, made a knot according to custom; but as there was still remaining an end of thread, instead of cutting it as usual with scissors, she had recourse to the candle, which immediately set fire to the whole cloth. Being terrified, she ran away, and abandoned the king, who was thus burnt alive in his own palace."

Eventually the quarrel resulted in (our) Charles plotting to have (the other) Charles assassinated; setting his own brother Philip, count of Longueville, and a bunch of hired thugs on the man's trail. Once they caught up with him, Philip said, "Charles of Spain, I am Philip, son of a king, whom you have foully slandered."

And then they beat him to death.

Leveraging his good relations with the English king Edward III, Charles got John to explicitly pardon him and his men for the murder of his constable a few months later. By the terms of this treaty (the Peace of Mantes), Charles also received substantial tracts in Normandy as compensation for the territories his mother had lost.

Over the course of the next two decades, Charles would be at the center of no less than ten different plots to dispossess the French Valois rulers, with the disastrous result that by A.D. 1379, Charles had been stripped of all of his French possessions, and barely held on to his crown.

★93★
POPE URBAN VI
Crazy Like a Pope
(CA. A.D. 1318–1389)

> He lacked Christian gentleness and charity. He was naturally
> arbitrary and extremely violent and imprudent, and when he
> came to deal with the burning ecclesiastical question of the day,
> that of reform, the consequences were disastrous.
> —*Ludwig Pastor*, History of the Popes

An orphan from the back alleys of Naples who rose through the ranks of
the Catholic Church through a combination of intelligence, hard work,
austerity, and honesty, Bartolomeo Prignano became Pope Urban VI to
the cheers of the Roman mob, who had called for a return to having Italian
popes ("or else!") after seventy years of French ones.

The only problem was that becoming Urban VI apparently drove the
previously mild-mannered Bartolomeo Prignano nuts.

Urban immediately began scolding the very cardinals who had elected him
about the need for reform, including discouraging them from accepting gifts,
such as cash annuities, from foreign dignitaries (a common practice in the
moldering swamp of corruption that was the late medieval church hierarchy).
Needless to say, this went over about as well as a fart in church.

Part of the problem was that Urban had never been a cardinal, only an
archbishop, and some of the cardinals who had been passed over were natu-
rally prone to be resentful.

A number of these cardinals (all of them French) met at Anagni and
invited the pope to meet with them to discuss their concerns. Smelling a
rat—it was entirely possible the cardinals would kidnap him, cart him off
to France, and force him to reign at Avignon—Urban stayed away. So these

same French cardinals took the extraordinary step of excommunicating him and nominating one of their number (Robert of Geneva) as Clement VII, who came to be called the anti-pope. The church was broken apart in a schism and stayed that way until A.D. 1417.

Having helped to cause the rift, Urban would not live to see it healed. During the twelve years of his pontificate he attempted (mostly futilely) to reassert the secular authority of the pope in the Italian peninsula. Most of the nobles there had grown used to running their own shows with minimal church interference during the seventy years that the papacy had been centered at Avignon. They resented Urban's attempt to turn back the clock.

By A.D. 1385, Urban found himself bottled up by opposing forces during a long siege in the Italian town of Nocera. While there, he imprisoned five of his cardinals for disloyalty. Dragging them along when he finally got clear of Nocera, Urban eventually sentenced these unfortunate men to death, having all but one of them either sewn up in burlap sacks and tossed into the sea or buried alive.

Four years later Urban joined these same men in death, leaving a divided Christendom and a chaotic situation in Italy.

Crazy bastard.

GOLDEN RULE

Before becoming pope, Archbishop Prignano was in charge of the collection of tithes for most of Italy. So he knew where the gold was collected from, where it was taken, and how it was spent. In the course of doing this job, he developed an uncanny head for business, something rare in late medieval church officials.

★94★

HENRY IV OF ENGLAND
Why You Should Be Nice
to Your Relatives
(A.D. 1366–1413)

King Henry would never have been king . . . if his cousin Richard
had treated him in the friendly manner he ought to have done.
— *Jean Froissart*, Chronicles

The son of John of Gaunt (himself the younger son of King Edward III),
Henry Bolingbroke, who held the titles duke of Hereford and earl of
Derby, was a peer of the realm, a cousin of the current King Richard II,
and an accomplished military man by the time he was suddenly exiled by
the king in A.D. 1398. Richard went on to seize all of Bolingbroke's lands
the following year, dispossessing him utterly and leaving him nearly pen-
niless. Before he was finished, Bolingbroke would famously make Richard
pay for this insult when he usurped the throne in A.D. 1399, deposing the
king and having himself crowned as Henry IV.

One of the Lords Appellant, a group of powerful nobles who pulled a power
play and forced the then-underage King Richard II to dismiss some of his more
tyrannical government ministers, Henry incurred Richard's wrath. Added to
this smoldering resentment was Richard's nagging suspicion that Henry had
designs on his crown.

But Henry was such a successful general in Richard's service (trained by
two of the best generals of the Middle Ages: his own father, John of Gaunt,
and his uncle, Edward the Black Prince) that his accomplishments couldn't
be ignored. Richard made him a duke in A.D. 1397, but, alarmed at Henry's
increasing popularity, banished him the very next year. When John of Gaunt

died in A.D. 1399, Richard seized all of his lands before Henry could inherit them.

That was the last straw for Henry. He returned from exile in France at the head of a tiny force of 300 men. At first he said that he was only interested in securing his inheritance. That changed, however, when thousands began to flock to his banner.

Within weeks, Richard, who at first cowered in hiding in Wales, was deposed and thrown into prison by Henry, who had himself crowned as King Henry IV. Having surrendered and agreed to abdicate in return for having his life spared, Richard was initially treated well. But once a plot to murder Henry came to light, Henry agreed that Richard was too dangerous alive, and murdered him by starving him to death, sometime in early A.D. 1400.

Henry thought such a move would secure the throne, but he was very much mistaken. Reigning for another thirteen years, he put down rebellion after rebellion until his health broke, and he was forced to look on nearly powerless as his son, Henry, prince of Wales (later King Henry V), took the reins of the kingdom, paving the way for his own subsequent and even more violent reign.

LEPROUS BASTARD?

Beginning in A.D. 1406, Henry IV began to exhibit symptoms of a wasting disease that may have been leprosy. At the time, people believed that leprosy was a punishment sent from God for egregious sin. Because Henry had executed the archbishop of York without trial on a charge of treason, there was widespread belief among his subjects that Henry's disease was just such a punishment. By the end of his life, Henry agreed with them.

HENRY V OF ENGLAND
Don't Let That Frat-Boy Act Fool Ya
(A.D. 1387–1422)

> As you have kept the crown by the sword, so will I keep it while my life lasts.
>
> —*Henry, Prince of Wales (future King Henry V) to his father, King Henry IV*

Despite what you may have gleaned from watching Shakespeare's play of the same name, King Henry V of England was not some dilettante, angst-ridden romantic initially acting out against daddy only to come to his senses on his father's death, turn all vice to virtue, and become some sort of all-wise warrior-philosopher king.

What he was, in fact, was the strong-minded son of a strong-minded father, raised, as Philip of Macedon had raised Alexander, with kingship and conquest in mind. While it's true that Henry had a wild youth, loved to party, and, upon becoming king, issued a decree that none of his drinking buddies were allowed to come within ten miles of him, it's not as if the guy turned into King Arthur.

First and foremost, Henry was (like his father before him) a soldier. The young prince was leading successful military campaigns against Welsh rebels in the English marches while still in his early teens. Like Richard the Lion-Hearted before him, Henry had a talent for war.

Upon taking the throne at age twenty-six in A.D. 1413, Henry let it be known that he intended to declare war on France unless he was immediately acknowledged the rightful king of France and heir to the throne. Henry pushed his admittedly flimsy claim (it was through his great-great-grandmother) because the French king, Charles VI, was apparently mad as a hatter. Henry's demands got him a good laugh across the Channel for his trouble, and he invaded France in A.D. 1415.

Striking quickly and making use of the longbowmen whose long-range "artillery" gave the English forces a decided tactical advantage over their French adversaries, Henry and his tiny army destroyed a French army nearly four times their size at the Battle of Agincourt later that year. On that day alone, 5,000 French knights died in the mud, shot from their saddles as they charged the English lines, dead before they could come within striking distance of the enemy.

In A.D. 1420, Henry parlayed this and several subsequent victories into a peace treaty with the French that called for him to be named regent for the now hopelessly insane Charles VI, to marry Charles's daughter, Catherine de Valois (more about her later), and to rule in the king's name. Also by terms of the treaty, Charles's son, the dauphin ("crown prince"), was dispossessed and disinherited.

— ∽ —

BATTLE-SCARRED BASTARD

In A.D. 1403, while fighting with his father against the forces of the Northumberland rebel Percy family, the sixteen-year-old Prince Henry was hit in the face by an arrow, with the point left lodged in his head. Luckily, his father had one of the most skilled doctors of the age in his service at the time. The doctor treated the injury with honey, removed the arrowhead, then doused the wound with alcohol before stitching it up. Left alive (the mortality rate for this sort of wound was high in the fifteenth century) but badly scarred, Henry fared better than Henry Percy, leader of the rebels, who was also hit in the face by an arrow during the same battle and killed instantly.

A harsh treaty imposed on a large and resourceful country. Because he had the bad grace to die of dysentery within two years of forcing it on the French, Henry left behind an infant son incapable of ruling on his own, and utter chaos in France. The result would be another thirty years of war, with a cost of untold millions in coin and countless lives.

And that can all be laid at the feet of that glorious bastard, Henry V.

★96★
TOMAS DE
TORQUEMADA
Grand Inquisitor, Closet Jew
(A.D. 1420–1498)

—The hammer of heretics, the light of Spain, the saviour of his
country, the honor of his order.
—*Medieval chronicler Sebastián de Olmedo*

Once synonymous with words like honor and duty, the name Torquemada
is now pretty much associated with fanaticism and torture. And it's all
due to the actions of one energetic man: Tomas de Torquemada, grand
inquisitor of Spain.

Born and raised in Valladolid, Torquemada began his life in religious service
as a cook-monk in a Dominican monastery. Over the next several decades, he
worked his way up through the order's ranks until he was named the private
chaplain of Isabella of Castile (the same queen who bankrolled Columbus's
voyage of discovery), and eventually grand inquisitor in A.D. 1483.

As such, Torquemada spearheaded the Spanish Catholic Church's crusade to enforce purity of belief. In this, he did not focus on cradle Catho-
lics, or unbelievers like Jews or Muslims. Instead, his passion was reserved
for ensuring those who had converted (conversos) to Roman Catholicism
remained good, orthodox Christians and didn't backslide. And if he had to
order a little waterboarding (they called it the "water cure"), or use of the
strappado (a leather strap used to lash a person's arms behind their back
from which they were hung, causing intense pain and dislocation of one or
both shoulders), or a turn of the rack, or the odd burning at the stake to
ensure this result, then it must be God's will, right?

There's a trend among modern historians to try to rehabilitate Torquemada's image, but the guy was a sadistic bastard, directly responsible for the torture of thousands, with many of his victims dying as a result of their interrogation. And more, he was an absolute hypocrite.

Why?

Because Tomas de Torquemada was Jewish!

Well, actually it was his great-grandparents who were. This according to a contemporary converso historian named Hernando de Pulgar, who wrote about Torquemada's uncle Juan: "his grandparents were of the lineage of Jews converted to our holy Catholic faith." In addition, at least one modern historian has asserted that one of Torquemada's grandmothers was also a convert.

To top it off, late in life, this nasty bastard was the driving force behind the Alhambra Decree, which expelled the Jews from Spain. There can be little doubt that numbered among the tens of thousands of Jews kicked out of Spain at Torquemada's request were many of his own blood relatives!

During his own lifetime, Torquemada became the focus of such hatred on the part of the Spanish people that he never went anywhere without a retinue of at least fifty hired bodyguards. After he died in A.D. 1498, he was buried with honors in what had been a Jewish cemetery before he had it seized and converted into the cemetery of a Dominican monastery he ordered built on the spot.

In A.D. 1832, liberals with sort of sense ironic humor that Torquemada so obviously lacked dug up his bones and burned them. Fiery bastard.

WHAT'S IN A NAME?

In one of history's great ironies, Torquemada was the nephew of a reforming Dominican friar named Juan de Torquemada, who wrote several well-respected tracts about the importance of religious tolerance to a healthy Catholic Church. In fact, this Torquemada was a leading defender of conversos throughout Spain, the very people his nephew later targeted for torture!

★97★
LOUIS XI OF FRANCE
The Spider King
(A.D. 1423–1483)

> If you can't lie, you can't govern.
> —*King Louis XI of France*

The son of King Charles VII, who had been dispossessed and disinherited by King Henry V of England, Louis spent his childhood and early adulthood witnessing his father's attempts to pry the English out of northern France (the king didn't even own Paris at the time!). By the time he came to the throne at age thirty-eight, he had learned the hard lesson that the French nobility could not be trusted, since they usually had their own agendas when it came to the distribution of power, and that there was nothing to be gained by ever keeping his word to them.

So he didn't.

Ever.

The result for the country of France turned out better than you might expect. Louis XI was the most successful king at adding territory to the realm since Philip Augustus, and wouldn't see his equal again until the accession of Louis XIV during the seventeenth century.

Once he became king, Louis immediately set about breaking the power of the nobles in France. So when Philip the Good, senile ruler of the massive duchy of Burgundy, contacted him about wanting to go on crusade (it was the fifteenth century; the kingdoms of Western Europe hadn't mounted a notable crusade in well over a century), Louis slyly offered to bankroll the enterprise, in return for a large slice of Philip's duchy, and a rewrite of the duke's will.

This brought Louis into conflict with Philip's son, a violent fellow known alternately as Charles the Bold, Charles the Rash, and Charles the Terrible, depending on who was talking about him. Convinced that Louis was attempting to steal his inheritance (he was right), Charles rebelled against the king, convincing a large number of French, Dutch, and Flemish nobles to join him.

Louis lost battle after battle to Charles (who was a brilliant general), but was able to string out the conflict (just as Philip Augustus had done time and again with the kings of England) until he finally got lucky: Charles was killed at the Battle of Nancy in A.D. 1477, and with his father's redrawn will still on the books, the duchy of Burgundy got split down the middle between his two heirs: Philip's daughter and Charles's old enemy, the Spider King himself, Louis of France.

Louis's luck continued to hold: in A.D. 1481, four years after the death of Charles the Bold/Rash/Terrible, the king's cousin (Charles IV, Duke of Anjou) died without living children, and the duke willed his large estate in southern France to the king. So when Louis himself died two years later at age sixty, he left his heirs a much-expanded France.

ↄ

WHAT'S IN A NAME?

Louis had many nicknames, including "le Prudent" and "the Spider." He earned both of these, as he was better with money than his somewhat feckless father, and like Philip Augustus preferred to gain through intrigue rather than through the naked exercise of military power.

★98★
POPE ALEXANDER VI
Chastity, Schmastity, I'm the Pope and My Son's Gonna Be a Cardinal
(A.D. 1431–1503)

> Now we are in the power of a wolf, the most rapacious perhaps that this world has ever seen. And if we do not flee, he will inevitably devour us all.
>
> —*Cardinal Giovanni de' Medici on hearing of the election of Rodrigo Borgia as pope*

One of the early Renaissance popes whose conduct exemplified the deep systemic corruption of the Catholic Church at the end of the Middle Ages, Alexander VI was a Borgia and is more famous today not for being pope, nor even for his many excesses, but for being father of the infamous Lucrezia and Cesare Borgia (yes, those Borgias).

Completely ignoring the prohibition against clergy having sex, Borgia had several mistresses, and at least four children by one of them, an Italian woman named Vanozza dei Cattanei. Elevating nepotism to an art form, he filled high-level papal government positions with family members (including his own son Cesare, whom he made a cardinal while still a teenager, even though the boy hadn't spent a single day as a priest).

Spanish-born Rodrigo Borja (later changed to the Italian spelling of "Borgia") followed his uncle to Rome when the latter became Pope Callixtus III in A.D. 1455. After that, his ascent through the hierarchy of the Catholic Church was rapid, culminating in his being elected pontiff in A.D. 1492.

Although a talented administrator (a welcome change from the incompetence of several of the most recent popes), Alexander VI was a debauchee of the first order.

Just one of many examples of the tenor of the depravity at Alexander's papal court was the so-called "Ballet of the Chestnuts," a theme party put on by Alexander's son Cesare (by this time a cardinal in the Catholic Church without ever having become a priest) in his apartments in the Palazzo Apostolico in Rome in A.D. 1501. Among the attendees: the pope (Cesare's daddy), a number of cardinals, and fifty prostitutes whose clothes were auctioned off, and who were then required to crawl around the floor on hands and knees, picking up hundreds of chestnuts dropped there for the purpose of getting these prostitutes on all fours and keeping them there. Every chestnut retrieved garnered the woman retrieving it a cash bonus.

And of course while they were down there, all those godly men in attendance got busy gettin' busy with them. Male orgasms were kept track of by an attendant, and the guy who had the most over the course of the party won the contest. The originator of the Orgasm Game? None other than Pope Alexander VI!

─────────────── ∽ ───────────────

THE TRUTH ABOUT THESE BORGIA BASTARDS

Lucrezia Borgia, one of history's great villainesses, gets a bad rap. Hardly the poison-brewing succubus contemporary chroniclers made her out to be, Lucrezia was a pious, God-fearing woman and, as far as we can tell, a loyal wife to her various husbands. The problem was her vicious brute of a brother Cesare, who killed indiscriminately in pursuit of ultimate power. Included among his victims: at least one of Lucrezia's husbands and one of his and Lucrezia's brothers!

RICHARD III OF ENGLAND
Hunchback? No. Child-Killer? Probably
(A.D. 1452–1485)

> I would my uncle would let me have my life
> though I lose my kingdom.
> —*King Edward V of England*

Made infamous by Shakespeare's play, Richard III of England has come down through history as a monster who seduced the widow of the rightful heir to the English throne in order to get at her immense wealth; set up his own brother to be tried and executed for treason against their eldest brother, Edward IV; and most notoriously usurped the throne on the death of the aforementioned brother/king, took his two nephews prisoner, and quietly had them murdered in the Tower of London once he'd secured his hold on the throne.

The youngest brother of King Edward IV, Richard, then duke of Gloucester, was one of Edward's most trusted advisors and generals by the time Edward consolidated his reign. After the rival claimant to the throne, Edward of Westminster, was killed in battle, Richard married his widow Anne Neville. This was no mean feat since Richard was rumored to have had a hand in killing her husband in the first place!

In A.D. 1483, when Edward IV died, Richard became regent for Edward's underaged sons. He moved quickly to secure physical control of the boys, managing to kidnap both of them and send them to "protective custody" in the Tower of London.

Next, Richard moved to have them declared illegitimate on the grounds that their father had been engaged to someone else when he secretly married their mother, Elizabeth Woodville, in A.D. 1463. His supporters on the regency council agreed with Richard that this was a clear case of bigamy, and that all of the dead king's children were illegitimate and therefore unable to succeed to the throne.

Just like that, Richard, duke of Gloucester, became Richard III, king of England. Neither of the princes was ever seen or heard from again. Some historians speculate that someone else did them in, but it doesn't make much sense for someone else to have killed the boys, because no one else could have profited from their deaths as much as their uncle.

Richard had precious little time to enjoy his ill-gotten crown, though. Within two years, he was facing open rebellion in the person of a distant cousin of the Lancaster kings, Henry Tudor, who landed in England at the head of a small army and was quickly joined by many of Richard's own lords. Attempting to put down this rebellion, Richard was killed at the Battle of Bosworth Field, the last English king to die in battle.

―――――――――― ◡◠ ――――――――――

HUNCHBACKED BASTARD?

Throughout his play *Richard III*, William Shakespeare consistently portrays the Duke of Gloucester and last Plantagenet king of England as a hunchback. There is no evidence from contemporary sources to support this claim, and it's pretty clear that Shakespeare was borrowing the notion from authors who wrote during the reign of Richard's successor Henry Tudor. These authors (including Shakespeare) curried favor with the Tudor monarch by vilifying Richard and representing Richard's alleged crooked spine as an outward manifestation of his inner villainy.

★100★
HENRY VII OF ENGLAND
The Cheap Bastard's Guide to Solidifying Your Hold on Power
(A.D. 1457–1509)

He was of a high mind, and loved his own will and his own way; as one that revered himself, and would reign indeed. Had he been a private man he would have been termed proud: But in a wise Prince, it was but keeping of distance; which indeed he did towards all; not admitting any near or full approach either to his power or to his secrets. For he was governed by none.

— *Sir Francis Bacon*

A distant cousin of the Lancastrian dynasty defeated by Edward IV, Henry Tudor was a young Welsh nobleman who bounced around Europe living mostly in exile until popping onto the scene in the early 1480s and challenging Richard III's hold on the English throne.

Once he'd seized power, Henry VII proved a capable, if ruthless, ruler. Determined to end nearly a century of civil war, he settled the succession question for decades to come by marrying a princess of the opposing York family. Not fond of crowds, suspicious of the nobility, and so tight with money that his wallet squeaked on the rare occasions when he opened it, Henry VII ruled for a quarter of a century unloved by his indifferent subjects, and died virtually unmourned by them as well.

Inheriting a realm bankrupted by decades of civil war, Henry early on hit on a number of ways to make ends meet with the nobility footing the bill. He staffed his retinue with nearly twice the number of retainers as any previous English king, then set up royal visits to his most wealthy landowners (most of them dukes and earls, guys with lots of land and lots of money). A "royal visit" consisted of Henry and his entire court descending on a given lord's country estate and staying there for from two weeks to a month, with the lord in question having the honor of feeding, housing, and entertaining the king and his retinue. This had the double effect of keeping his greatest nobles too poor to fund rebellions against him, and of saving the crown itself an awful lot of money!

--------------------------------- ∽ ---------------------------------

DOUBLY A BASTARD!

Henry Tudor's blood connection to the royal House of Lancaster was twofold: on the one hand, his grandfather, Owain Tudor, a squire serving in the Lancaster household, secretly married Catherine of Valois, the widow of Henry V. She had four children by Tudor before the marriage was annulled (with the result that all four of their children were declared illegitimate) and Tudor was thrown into prison for a time. One of Owain's sons by this liaison, Edmund Tudor, grew up to marry Lady Margaret Beaufort. For her part, Margaret was the great-granddaughter of John of Gaunt, Edward III's younger son, who was also father of the future king Henry IV. Her grandfather was the first of four illegitimate children John of Gaunt had with his then-mistress and future wife Katherine Swynford. Both of Henry Tudor's blood claims to the throne of England came to him through illegitimate lines (although in the case of the Beauforts, that line was later declared legitimate by king and parliament), so this English king was quite literally doubly a bastard!

Another way in which Henry filled the kingdom's coffers was through marrying his eldest son Arthur to a wealthy Spanish princess named Catherine of Aragon, who brought with her a peace treaty with Spain and an enormous dowry. When Arthur died suddenly shortly after the wedding, Henry, rather than return the girl and her dowry to her father, simply got a dispensation from the pope and prepared to marry her off to his second son, Henry. As we shall see in the final chapter, this move, a money-saving gesture, had far-reaching unintended consequences of its own!

> We thought that the clergy of our realm had been our subjects
> wholly, but now we have well perceived that they be but half our
> subjects, yea, and scarce our subjects: for all the prelates at their con-
> secration make an oath to the Pope, clean contrary to the oath that
> they make to us, so that they seem to be his subjects, and not ours.
> —*King Henry VIII of England*

It is fitting that we close out our study of ancient bastards with a quick look at this last of the truly medieval monarchs. After Henry, no king of England would ever have so much license to do as he pleased.

The second son of Henry VII, young Henry didn't become heir to the throne until the age of ten. He succeeded his father at age eighteen, and inherited a well-ordered realm with a full treasury, thanks to his penny-pinching, reclusive father's programs as king. When he died thirty-eight years later, Henry would leave a vastly different England to his own heirs: a bankrupt treasury, a different official state religion, and (the last thing he wanted) a simmering succession crisis.

How he got there is an interesting story that could fill dozens of volumes (and has). For starters, chalk it up to the parsimony of his father: Henry VII had married his son Arthur to Catherine of Aragon, the daughter of the king of Spain, in return for a huge amount of gold and silver. When Arthur died four months after the marriage, Henry refused to return Catherine or the money. The crisis was resolved when Henry VIII took the throne, got the pope's blessing to marry his brother's widow, and did so that same year.

The problem was that Catherine couldn't give him a male heir. Only one of their children lived to adulthood: Mary (the future "Bloody Mary"). So Henry decided to divorce her and marry someone else who could give him the heir he desperately wanted.

The only problem was that there was a different pope by this time, a pope who owed his throne to the most powerful king in Europe: Charles V Hapsburg, king of Spain and the Holy Roman Emperor. And Charles V just happened to be the beloved nephew of the woman that Henry now wished to set aside.

So the pope said no. And Henry, who had actually been named "Defender of the Faith" for writing a tract excoriating the new Protestant sects in Germany, did the unthinkable: he broke with the Catholic Church, founded the Church of England, with himself as its head, dissolved the monasteries in England (pocketing both their property and their wealth), and began marrying a series of women intended to give him a male heir.

Purposeful bastard.

BASTARD AND HIS WIVES

In the end, Henry had six wives (and an untold number of mistresses, including the sister of one of these wives). Two of his wives were beheaded for "treason" (adultery committed by a queen was considered treason at the time, and they were accused adulterers), and one died giving him the only legitimate male child who lived past infancy (his successor, Edward VI). Only two of them, Anne of Cleves, whom he divorced, and Catherine Parr, his last queen, outlived him.

By the time of Henry's death, even the notion of monarchy was changing. The question of male heirs became ever-more irrelevant. In fact, Henry did sire arguably the greatest monarch ever to rule England, an effective, diligent, intelligent ruler who outfoxed every opponent and made England a player on the modern stage in ways of which Henry could have only dreamed.

It's unlikely that this royal bastard even considered the possibility that the heir he so desired would actually be a woman, and a great one.

Elizabeth I—in many ways an even bigger (and more effective) bastard than her old man.

How's that for a "modern" notion?

INDEX

A

Acre, Battle of, 178–80
Adalgis, 146
Aelfgifu, 156, 157
Aemilianus, Scipio, 51, 52
Aethelgifu, 156
Agincourt, Battle of, 217
Agnes of Merania, 189
Agrippa, Marcus, 104
Agrippina, 109–10, 114–15
Akhenaton, 6–8
Alcibiades, 27–28
Alcmeonid family, 22, 28
Alexander the Great, 37–43, 54–55
Alexander VI, Pope, 223–24
Alfred the Great, 156
Alhambra Decree, 220
Alienus, Aulus Caecina, 121
Alleghieri, Dante, 199
Alys of France, 171
Amenhotep III, 6
Amenhotep IV, 6–8
Amyntas IV, 35
Anna, 155
Anne of Cleves, 231
"Antiochus Epimanes," 49
"Antiochus Epiphanes," 49
Antiochus III, 48–49
Antiochus IV, 48–49, 58
Antiochus VIII, 53
Antiochus IX, 53
Antoninus, Marcus Aurelius, 133–34.
    See also Elagabalus
Antonius, Antyllus, 102
Antonius, Marcus, 60, 86–87, 98–102
Aper, Arrius, 137, 138

Appian, 53, 56, 65, 76
Aquillius, Manius, 56
Aristagoras, 24–26
Arnulf, King, 150
Arsinoe, 46–47
Arsuf, Battle of, 180
Arthur, son of Henry VII, 228, 230
Augusta, 131
Augustus, Aurelius Commo-
    dus Antoninus, 125. See also
    Commodus
Augustus, Philip, 172, 179, 183–84,
    186, 188–90
Augustus, Tiberius Caesar, 104–11
Aurelius, Marcus, 125

B

Bacon, Sir Francis, 227
Balas, Alexander, 53
Bardas, 152–53
Basil I, 152–53
Basil II, 154–55
Bassianus, Varius Avitus, 133. See also
    Elagabalus
Bathsheba, 15
Battle of Acre, 178–80
Battle of Agincourt, 217
Battle of Arsuf, 180
Battle of Bedriacum, 120–21
Battle of Bosworth Field, 226
Battle of Bouvines, 191
Battle of Hastings, 161
Battle of Lewes, 195
Battle of Nancy, 222
Battle of the Milvian Bridge, 140

Beaufort, Margaret, 228
Bedriacum, Battle of, 120–21
Belisaurius, 144, 145
Belshazzar, 16, 17
Benedict IX, Pope, 158–60, 181, 199
Berengaria, 179
Blagdon, Francis, 210
Blanche of Bourbon, 206
"Bloody Mary," 230
Bolingbroke, Henry, 214–15
Boniface VIII, Pope, 198, 199
Borgia, Cesare, 223, 224
Borgia, Lucrezia, 223, 224
Borgia, Rodrigo, 223
Borja, Rodrigo, 223
Bosworth Field, Battle of, 226
Bouvines, Battle of, 191
Browning, Robert, 150
Brutus, Lucius Junius, 61, 62
Brutus, Marcus Junius, 62, 95–98

C

"Cadaver Synod," 151
Caepoinis, Servilia, 96
Caesar, Augustus, 102, 104, 106. See
    also Octavian, Gaius Julius Caesar
Caesar, Gaius Julius, 59, 62, 68, 86,
    91–99, 101, 105, 112, 114
Caesar, Julia, 101
Caesar, Tiberius Augustus, 106–7
Caesarion, 59, 102
Caligula, 107, 110–12, 143
Cambyses, King, 18, 19, 20, 21
Caracalla, 131–32
Carinus, 135–36

Carloman, 146–47
Carus, 137, 139
Cassius, Gaius, 97–98
Catherine of Aragon, 230–31
Catiline, Lucius Sergius, 71–73, 99
Cato the Elder, 93
Cato the Younger, 93–94
Cattanei, Vanozza dei, 223
Cerda, Charles de la, 210
Cethegus, Cornelius, 76–78
Charlemagne, 146–47
Charles IV of France, 222
Charles VI of France, 216–17
Charles VII of France, 221
Charles the Bad, of Navarre, 209–11
Charles the Terrible, 221–22
Chlorus, Constantius, 141
Cicero, Marcus Tullius, 72–73, 86–88,
    90, 99, 102
Cinna, Lucius Cornelius, 74–75
Claudius, 112–14
Cleisthenes, 28
Clement V, Pope, 198–200
Cleopatra II, 51
Cleopatra VII, 58–60
Cleopatra Thea, 53–54
Cleopatra, Queen of Egypt, 100, 102
Commodus, 110, 125–26, 130, 143
Conrad, 166
Constantia, 141
Constantine the Great, 140–42
Constantine VI, Emperor, 149
Constantine VIII, 154
Constantius II, 142–43
Conti, Lotario dei, 181
Crassus, Marcus Licinius, 82–83

Crispus, 141
Critias, 29–31
The Critias, 29
Crusades, 168–70, 181
Curio, Gaius Scribonius, 100
Curthose, Robert, 162
Cyclops, 34
Cyrus the Great, 17

D

Dandolo, Enrico, 169–70
Dante, 199
Darius I, King, 23, 25
Darius I, King of Persia, 18–19
David, King, 14, 15
Demetrius II, 53
DeMille, Cecil B., 2
DeMolay, Jacques, 198, 200
Desiderius, King, 146, 147, 159
Despenser, Edward le, 203
Despenser, Hugh le, 202
"Devil's Brood," 171, 173, 183–85
Dio, Cassius, 100, 120, 128, 129, 133
Diocles, Gaius Aurelius Valerius, 137
Diocletian, 135–39
Dionysius I, 32–34
Dives, Marcus Licinius Crassus, 82–83
Dolabella, Gnaeus Cornelius, 88, 89
Domitian, 123–24, 143
Domus Aureum, 115
Drusilla, Livia, 104–5, 111
Drusus, 104–5, 109
Dunstan, Abbot, 156, 157

E

Eadwig, 156–57
Edmund I, 156
Edward I, King, 193–96, 201
Edward II, King, 201–4
Edward III, King, 204, 214, 228
Edward IV, King, 225
Edward V, King, 225
Edward VI, King, 231
Edward of Westminster, 225
Edward the Black, 205, 214
Edward the Confessor, 161
Einhard, 146
Elagabalus, 110, 133–34
Eleanor of Aquitaine, 171–74, 178, 183
Elizabeth I, 231
Elizabeth II, 206

F

Fausta, 141
Felix, Lucius Cornelius Sulla, 69–70
First Crusade, 168
Formosus, 150–51
Fourth Crusade, 169–70, 181
Froissart, Jean, 205, 207, 209, 214
Fulvia, 100

G

Galba, Servius Sulpicius, 117–19, 121
Galeazzo, Gian, 207–8
Galerius, 138
Gaveston, Piers, 202, 203
Geoffrey II of Brittany, 183–84

Gerald of Wales, 178, 179, 183, 188
Gerberga, 147
Germanicus, Nero Claudius Caesar
    Augustus, 109, 114. *See also* Nero
Geta, 131–32
Godwinson, Harold, 161
"Golden House," 115
Gouth, Raymond Bertrand de, 199
Gratianus, Johannes, 159
Green, Peter, 45
Gregory VI, Pope, 159
Gregory VII, Pope, 165–66
Gryffudd, Llewellyn Ap, 195

H

"Hammer of the Scots," 194, 196
Hammurabi, 4–5
Hammurabi's Code, 4–5
Hannibal of Carthage, 64–65
Hapsburg, Charles V, 231
Hastings, Battle of, 161
Helena, 141
Henry III, Emperor, 159
Henry IV, Emperor, 165–66
Henry VI, Emperor, 190
Henry II, King, 171–73, 178, 183
Henry III, King, 175, 192–93, 202
Henry IV, King, 214–15, 228
Henry V, King, 215–18, 221, 228
Henry VII, King, 227–30
Henry VIII, King, 136, 230–32
Henry the Lion, 190
Henry the Young King, 175–77
Herleva, 161
Herodian, 134

Herodotus, 19, 20, 24
Hezekiah, King, 12–13
Hippias, 22–23, 26, 28
Histiaeus, 25
The Historia Augusta, 136
Hood, Robin, 185
Hortensius, 94
Hruodgaus, 146
Hyparchus, 22

I

Innocent III, Pope, 181–82, 190–91
"Ionian Revolt," 19, 23–24, 26
Irene, Empress, 148–49
Isabella of Angouleme, 193, 202, 203
Isabella of Castile, 219

J

John I of England, 171–73, 175, 185–87, 189–90, 192
John of Gaunt, 205, 214–15, 228
John the Good, 209–10
Julian, 143
Julianus, Didius, 127–28
Justinian, 144–45

K

Keraunos, Ptolemy, 45–47
Knights Templar, 197–200

L

Lackland, John, 185
Lactantius, 137
Laodice, 49
Lentulus, Publius Cornelius, 99
Leo IV, Emperor, 148
Leopold V, Archduke, 179
Lewes, Battle of, 195
Licinianus, 141
Licinius, 141
The Lion in Winter, 179
Livy, 48, 61, 62
Lombards, 146–47
Long, Huey, 165
Longinus, Gaius Cassius, 97–98
Longshanks, Edward, 193–96, 201
Louis VII of France, 171–73, 188
Louis XI of France, 221–22
Lucan, 93
Lucretia, 62
Lusignans, 193
Lysandra, 45–46
Lysimachus, 45–46

M

Maccabee, Judah, 50
Macedonian Dynasty, 152–53
Macro, 107
Magna Carta, 187, 193
Magnus, Gnaeus Pompeius, 84–85
Manlius, 72, 73
Marcelinus, Ammianus, 143
Marcia, 126
Marius, Gaius, 66–68, 89
"Marius's Mules," 67

Marshall, William, 175, 176
Martial, 119
Maslow, Abraham, 194
Maud of Saint-Valery, 186
Maxentius, 141
Maximian, 141
McLynn, Frank, 190
Medici, Giovanni de', 223
Messalina, 113
Michael III, 152–53
Milvian Bridge, Battle of, 140
Mithridates VI of Pontus, 55–57
Montfort, Simon de, 194
Mortimer, Geoffrey, 203
Mortimer, Roger, 203–4

N

Nabonidus, King, 16–17
Nancy, Battle of, 222
Narses, 144, 145
Nero, 109, 114–17, 119, 121, 126
Neville, Anne, 225
Norwich, John Julius, 148, 154, 169
Numerian, 137–38

O

Octavia, 100
Octavian, Gaius Julius Caesar, 60,
   86–87, 98–106. *See also* Caesar,
   Augustus
Odo of Bayeux, 163–64
Olmedo, Sebastián de, 219
Olympias of Macedonia, 37, 39–41
Olympic Games, 40, 116

Otho, Marcus Salvius, 119–20
Otto IV of Germany, 190–91

P

Padilla, Maria de, 206
Parr, Catherine, 231
Pastor, Ludwig, 212
Paterculus, Velleius, 55
Pedro of Castile, 205–6
Pepin, King, 146
Percy, Henry, 217
Perdiccas II, 35
Pericles, 28
Pertinax, 127, 128
Peter of Wakefield, 186
Petrarch, 208
Philip II Augustus of France, 172, 179, 183–84, 186, 188–90
Philip II of Macedonia, 35–39, 43
Philip IV the Fair, 197–200
Philip VI of France, 209
Philip of Macedon, 216
Philip of Swabia, 190
Philip the Good, 221
Philoxenus, 33–34
Pindarus, 98
Pisistratus, 22
Pius, Marcus Aurelius Severus Antoninus, 132. *See also* Caracalla
Plantagenet, Geoffrey, 183–84
Plantagenet, Henry, 171–73
Plantagenet, John, 185–87
Plantagenet, Matilda, 190
Plantagenet, Richard, 178–80
Plato, 29, 32

Plautianus, Gaius Fulvius, 131
Pliny the Younger, 124
Plutarch, 39, 74, 86, 94, 98, 99
Polycrates, 20–21
Pompey the Great, 72, 84–85, 94, 96
Popilius, 48–49
Postumus, Agrippa, 105
Prignano, Bartolomeo, 212–13
"Prince of Wales," 195, 201
Ptolemy I Soter, 42–43, 45, 59
Ptolemy V, 51
Ptolemy VI, 53
Ptolemy VII, 51
Ptolemy VIII, 51–52
Ptolemy Keraunos (Thunderbolt), 45–47
Ptolemy Memphitis, 52
Pulcher, Publius Clodius, 79–81
Pulgar, Hernando de, 220

R

Ralph of Diceto, 175
Ramesses II, 9–11
Richard II, King, 214–15
Richard III, King, 225–26
Richard III, 225, 226
Richard I the Lion-Hearted, 171, 173, 177–80, 185–86, 188–89
Richard of Gloucester, 225–26
Robert I of Normandy, 161, 168
Rome, burning, 114, 115
Rufus, Quintus Curtius, 37
Runciman, Steven, 170

S

Sabinus, Flavius, 122
Saladin, 179–80
Sargon II, 12
Sargon of Akkad, 1–3
Savoyards, 192–93
Sejanus, Lucius Aelius, 106–9
Seleucus, 45–46, 53
Seleucus IV, 48–49
Seleucus V, 53–54
Seneca, 114
Sennacherib, King Of Assyria, 12–13
Severus, Septimius, 128–32
Shakespeare, William, 4, 60, 97, 216, 225–26
Siculus, 32, 42
Socrates, 27, 29
Solomon, King, 14–15
"Spider King," 221–22
Stephen VI, Pope, 150–51, 181
Stone of Scone, 196
Suetonius, 110, 112–13, 118, 120, 122–23
Suidas, 22, 23
Sulla, Lucius Cornelius, 69–70
Sulpicianus, 128
Swynford, Katherine, 228
Sylvester III, Pope, 159
"Synod Horrenda," 151

T

Tacitus, 104, 106, 108, 114–15, 117, 121, 124
Tarquinius, Sextus, 62–63
Tarquinius Superbus, Lucius, 61–63

Templars, 197–200
Theodora, 144, 145
Theophano, 154
Theramenes, 29–31
Thucydides, 27
Thurinus, Gaius Octavius, 102. See also Octavian, Gaius Julius Caesar
Tiberius, 104–11
Torquemada, Juan de, 220
Torquemada, Tomas de, 219–20
Tudor, Edmund, 228
Tudor, Henry, 226–28
Tudor, Owain, 228
Tullia, 61
Tzimiskes, John, 154

U

Urban VI, Pope, 212–13
Uticensis, Marcus Porcius Cato, 93–94

V

Valens, Fabius, 121
Valois, Catherine de, 217, 228
Vercingetorix, 91–92
Verres, Gaius, 87–90
Vespasian, 122, 123
Victor III, Pope, 159, 166
Visconti, Bernabò, 207–8
Visconti, Galeazzo, 207–8
Visconti, Matteo, 207–8
Vitellius, Aulus, 120–22
Vladimir I, 155

W

William I, King, 162, 163
William II (Rufus), 164, 167–68
William of Nogaret, 199
William the Conqueror, 161–62, 167
Woodville, Elizabeth, 226

X

Xenophon, 29, 30

DAILY BENDER

Want Some More?

Hit up our humor blog, The Daily Bender, to get your fill of all things funny—be it subversive, odd, offbeat, or just plain mean. The Bender editors are there to get you through the day and on your way to happy hour. Whether we're linking to the latest video that made us laugh or calling out (or bullshit on) whatever's happening, we've got what you need for a good laugh.

If you like our book, you'll love our blog. (And if you hated it, "man up" and tell us why.) Visit The Daily Bender for a shot of humor that'll serve you until the bartender can.